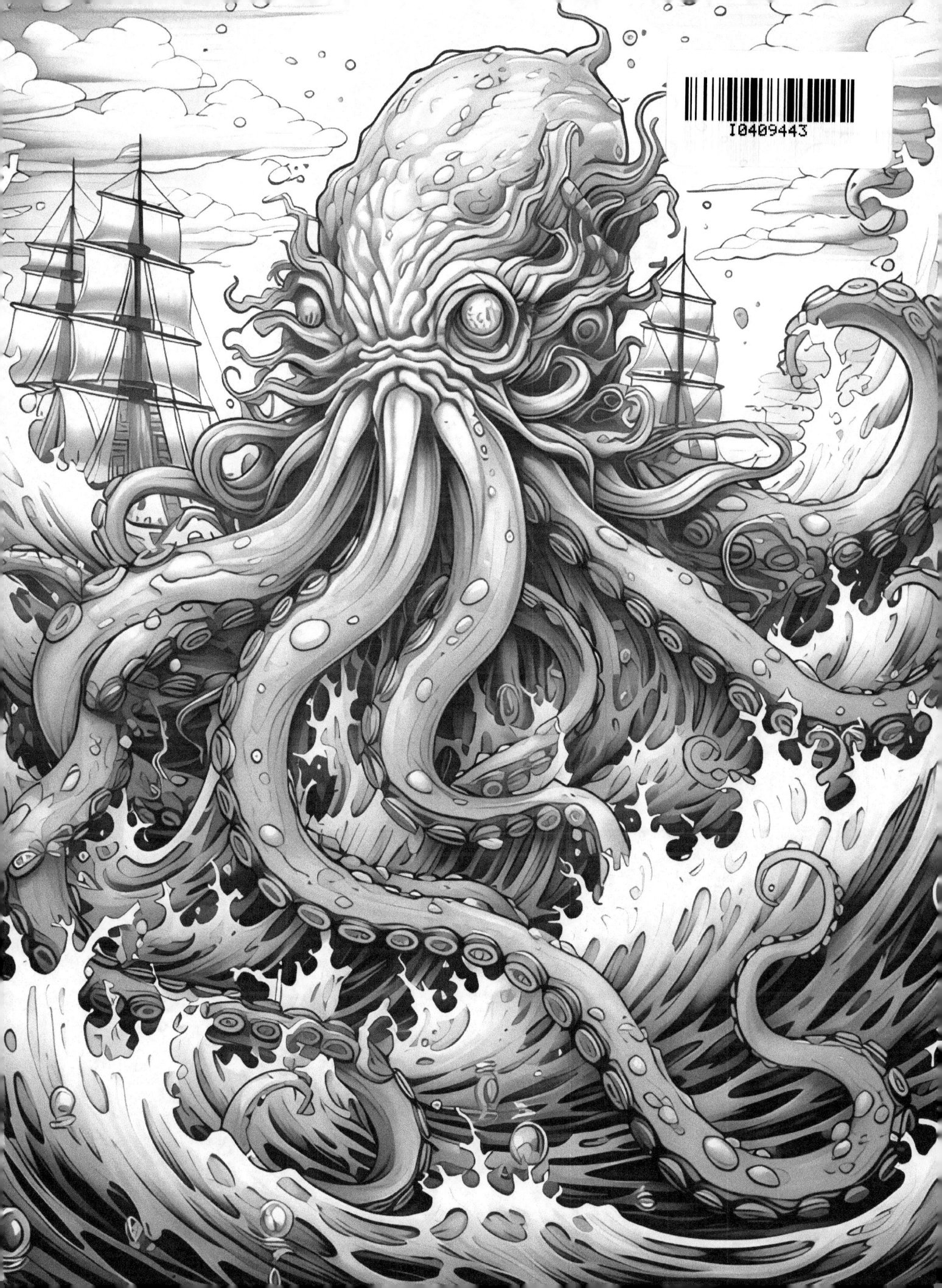

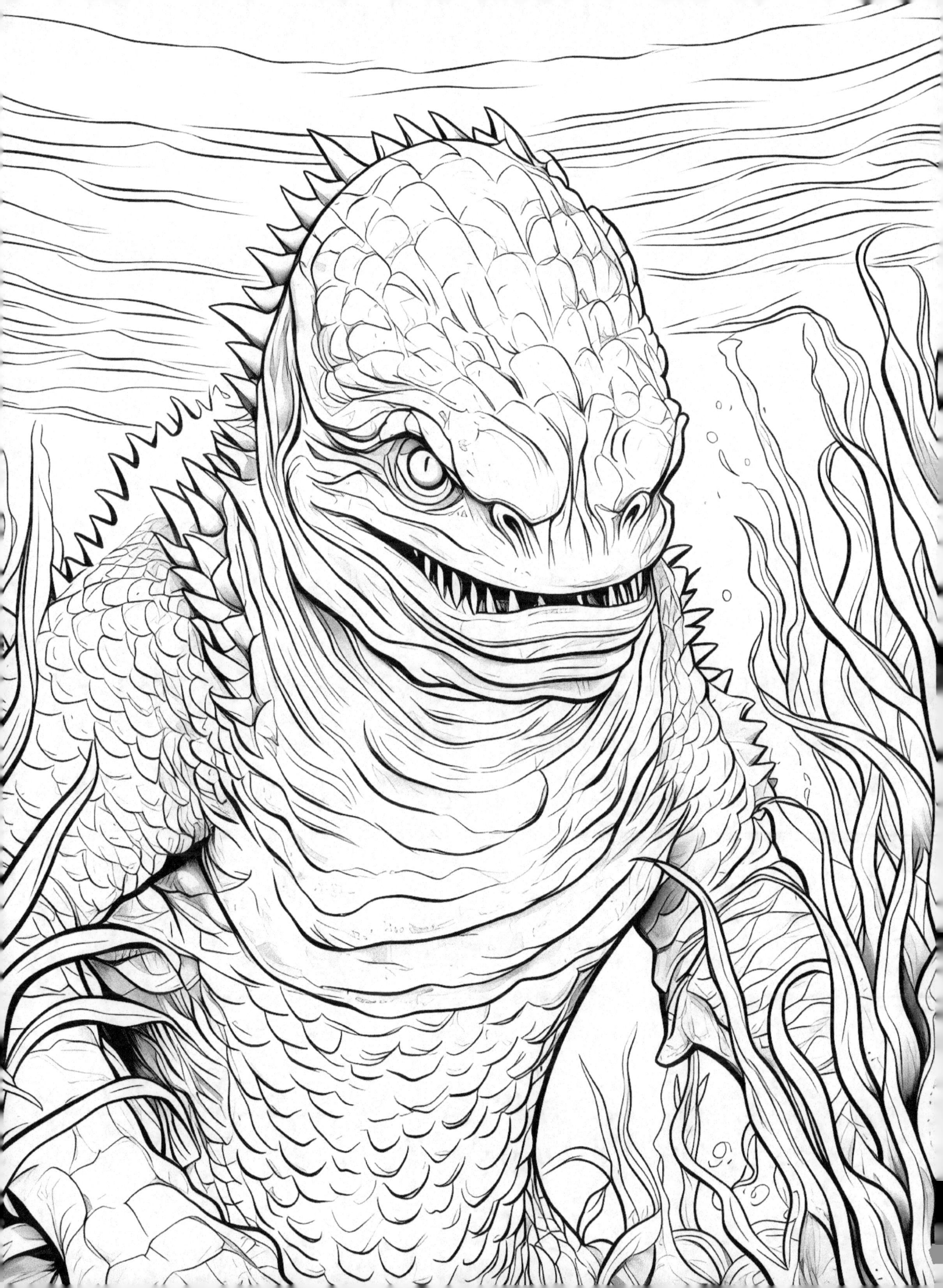

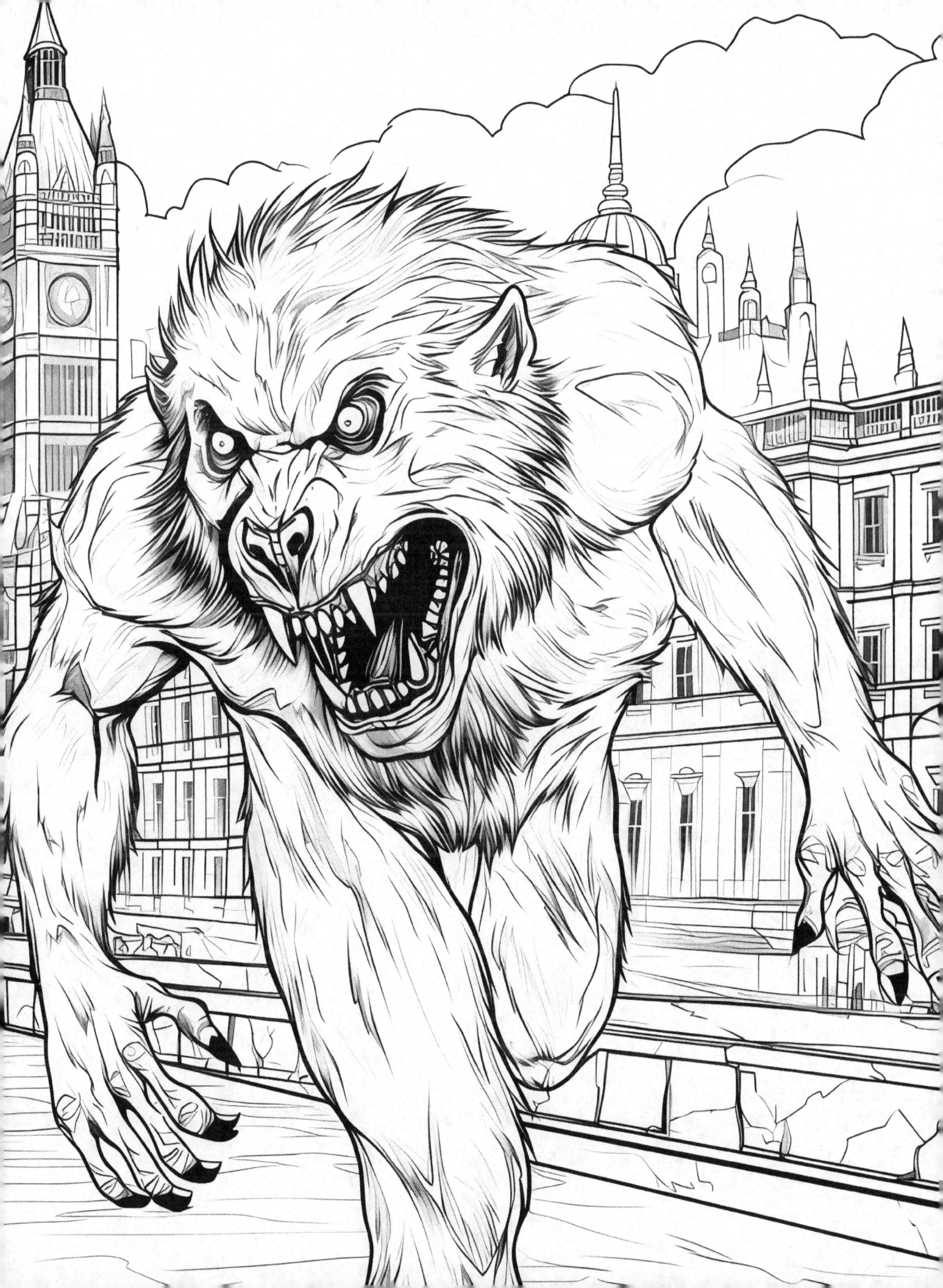

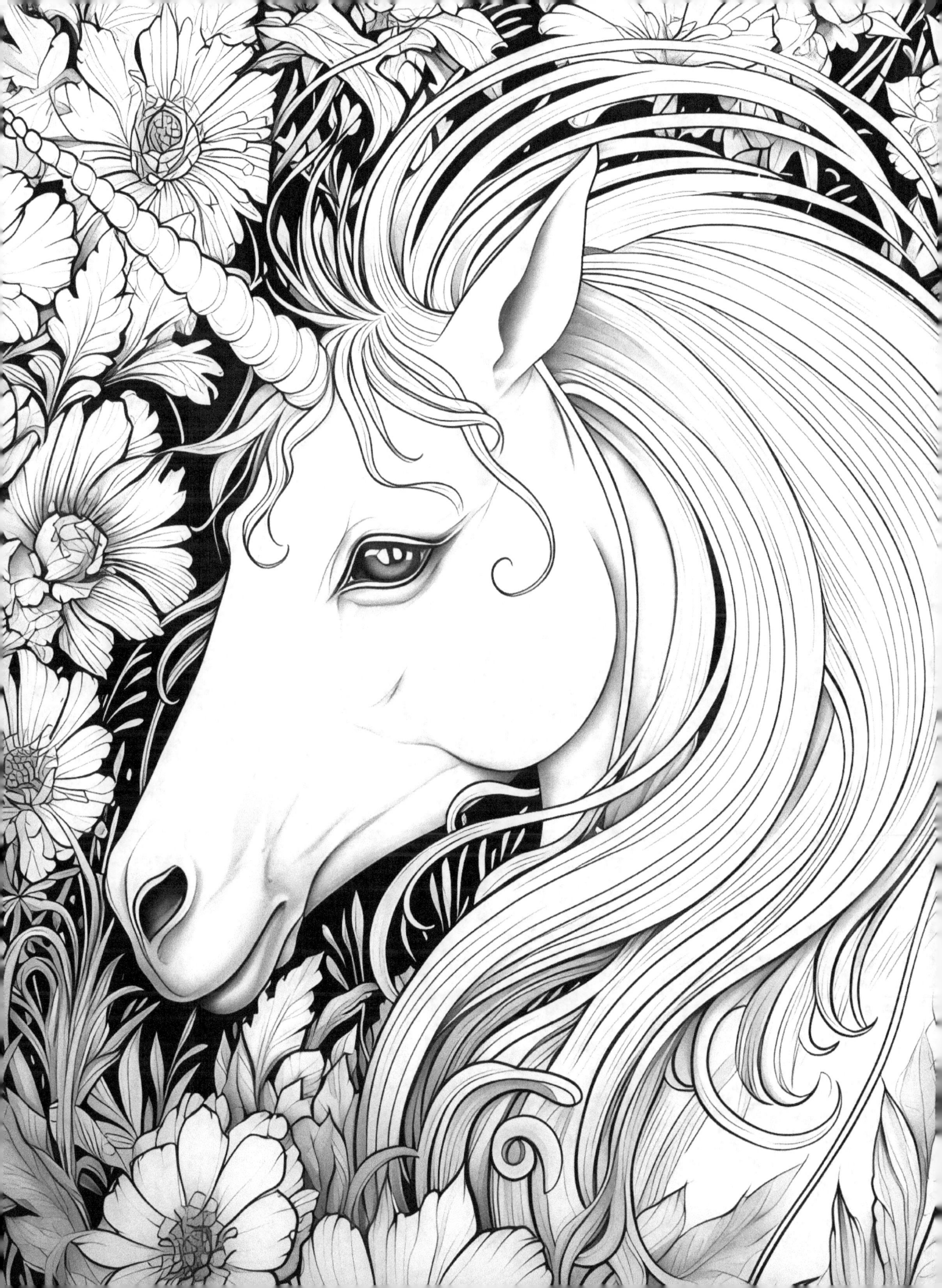

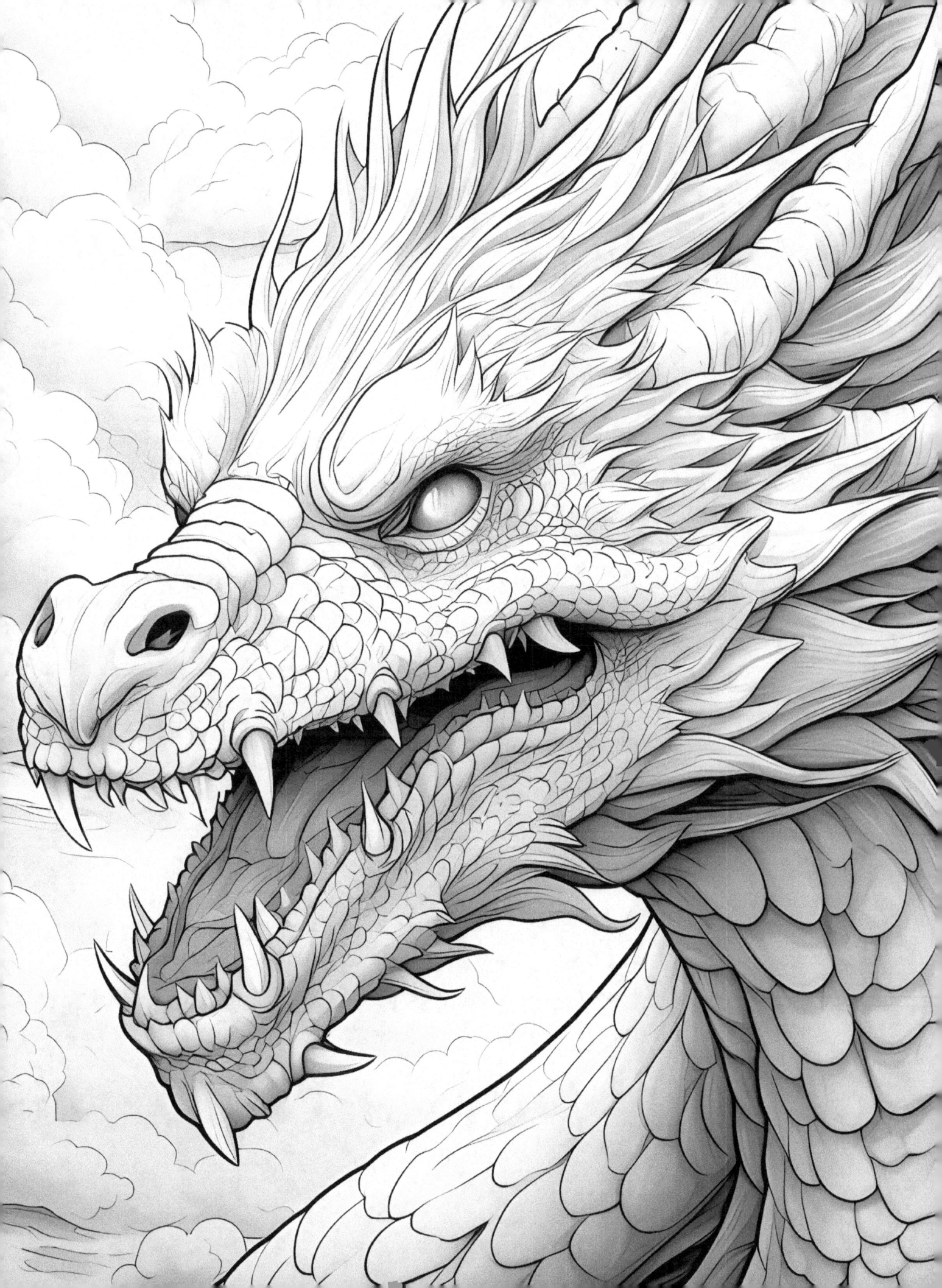

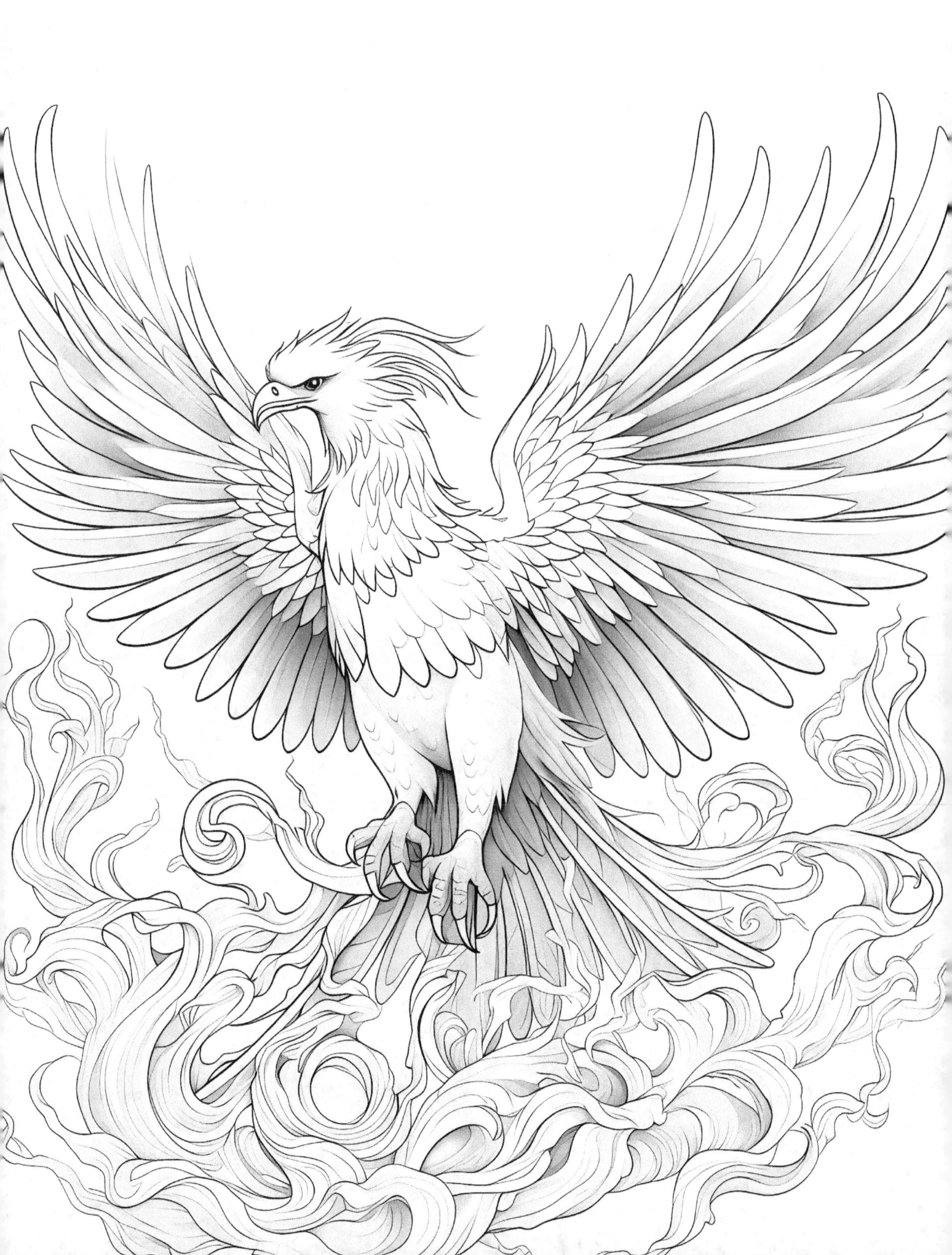

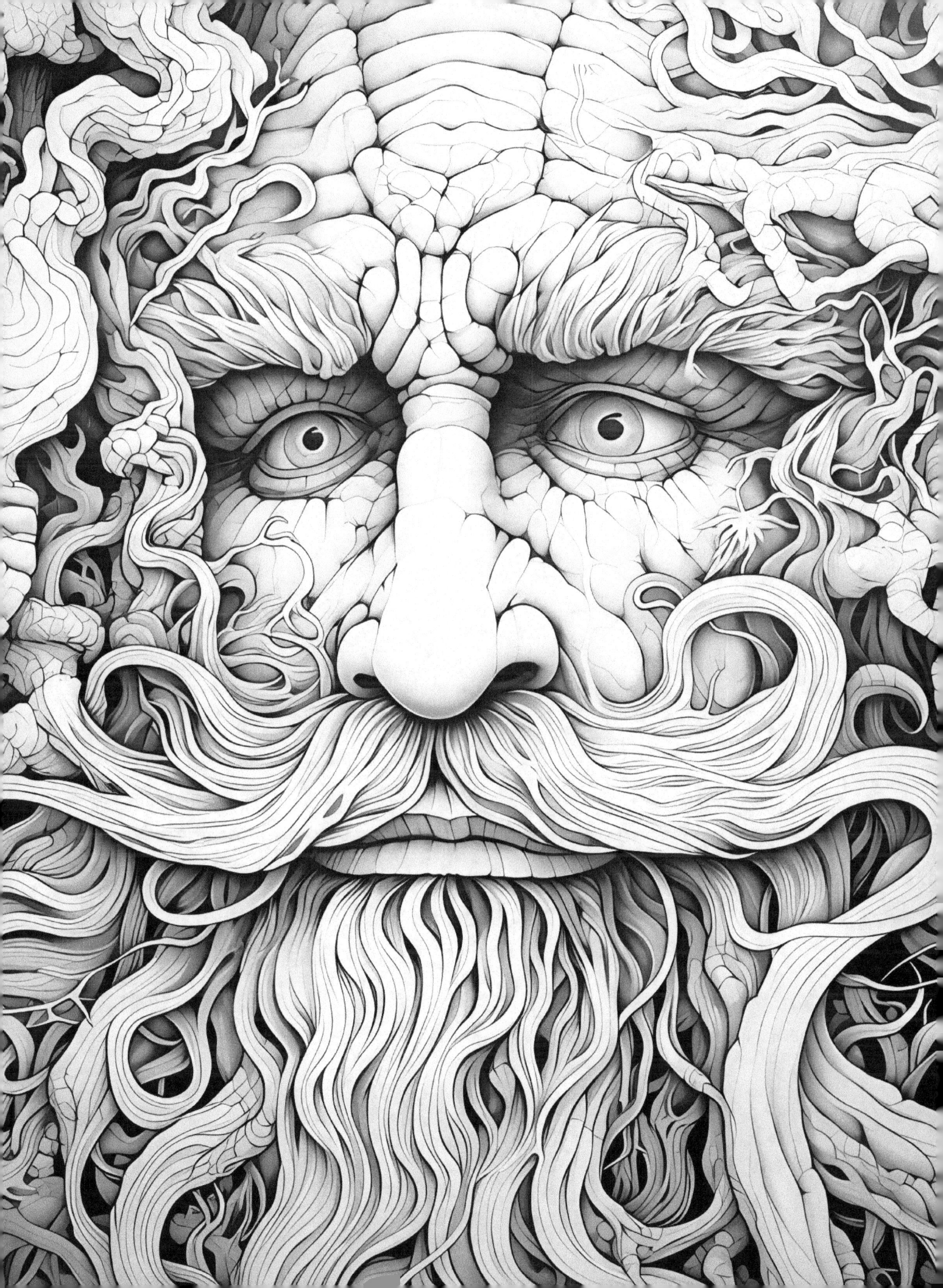

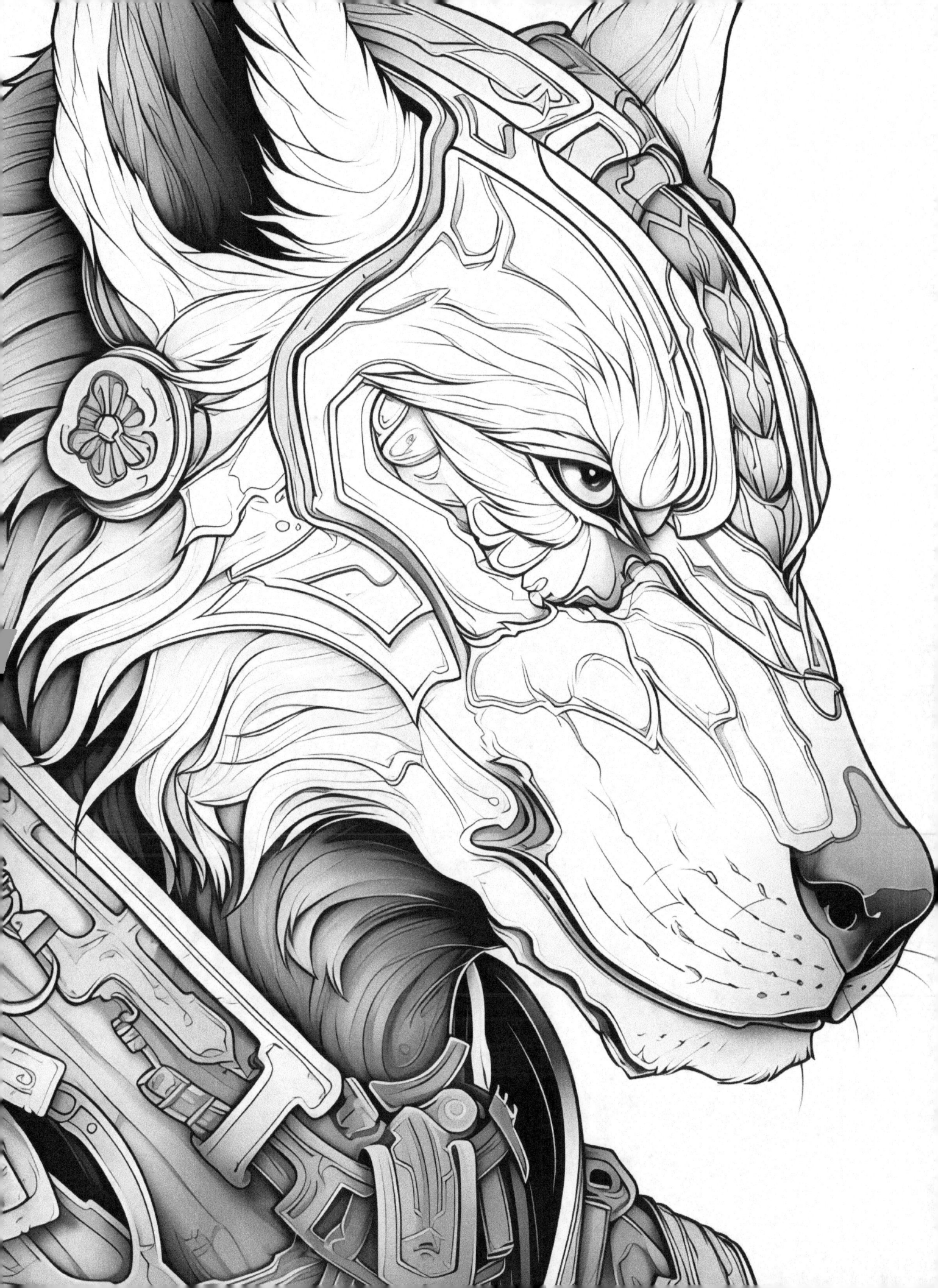

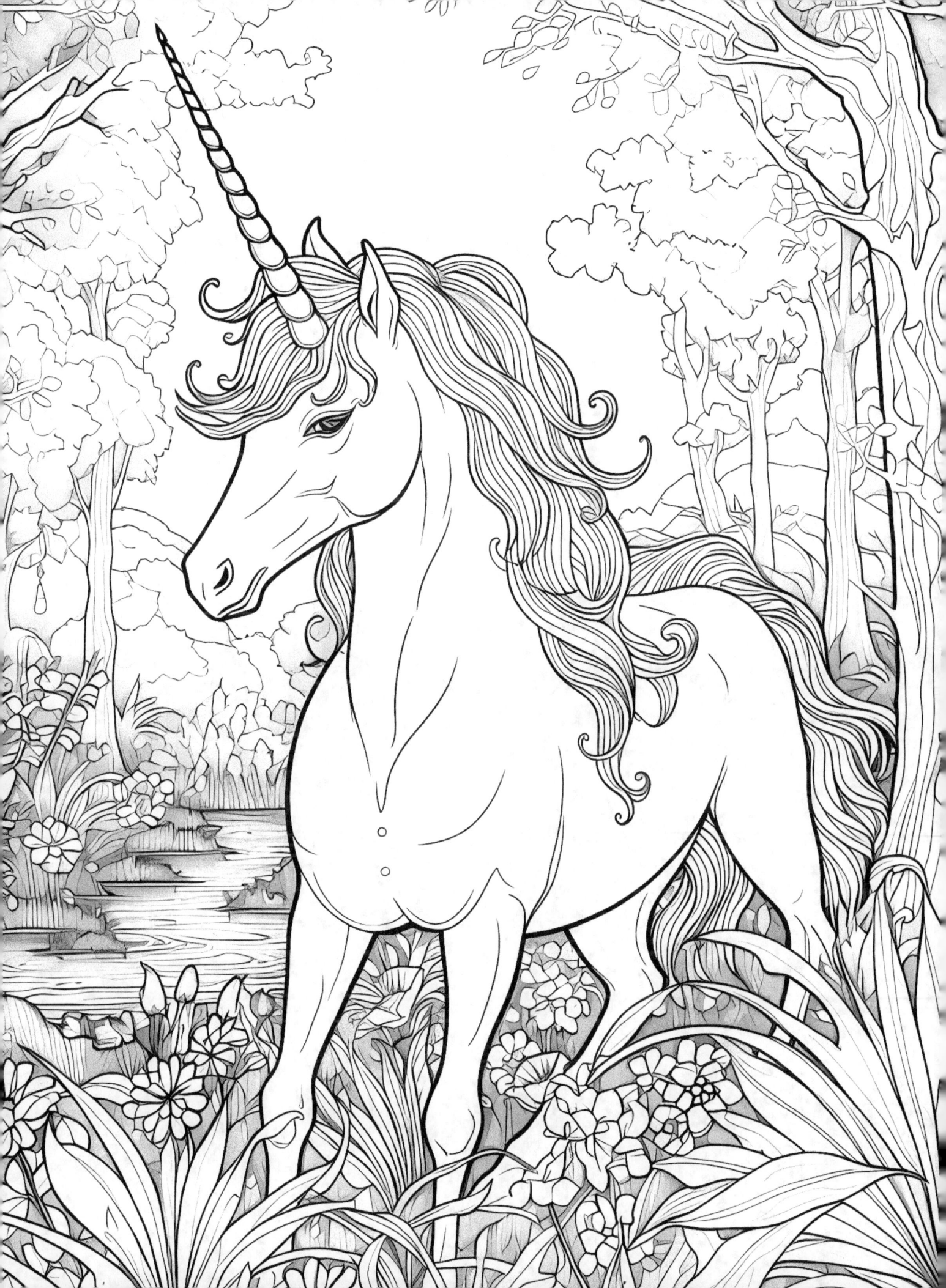

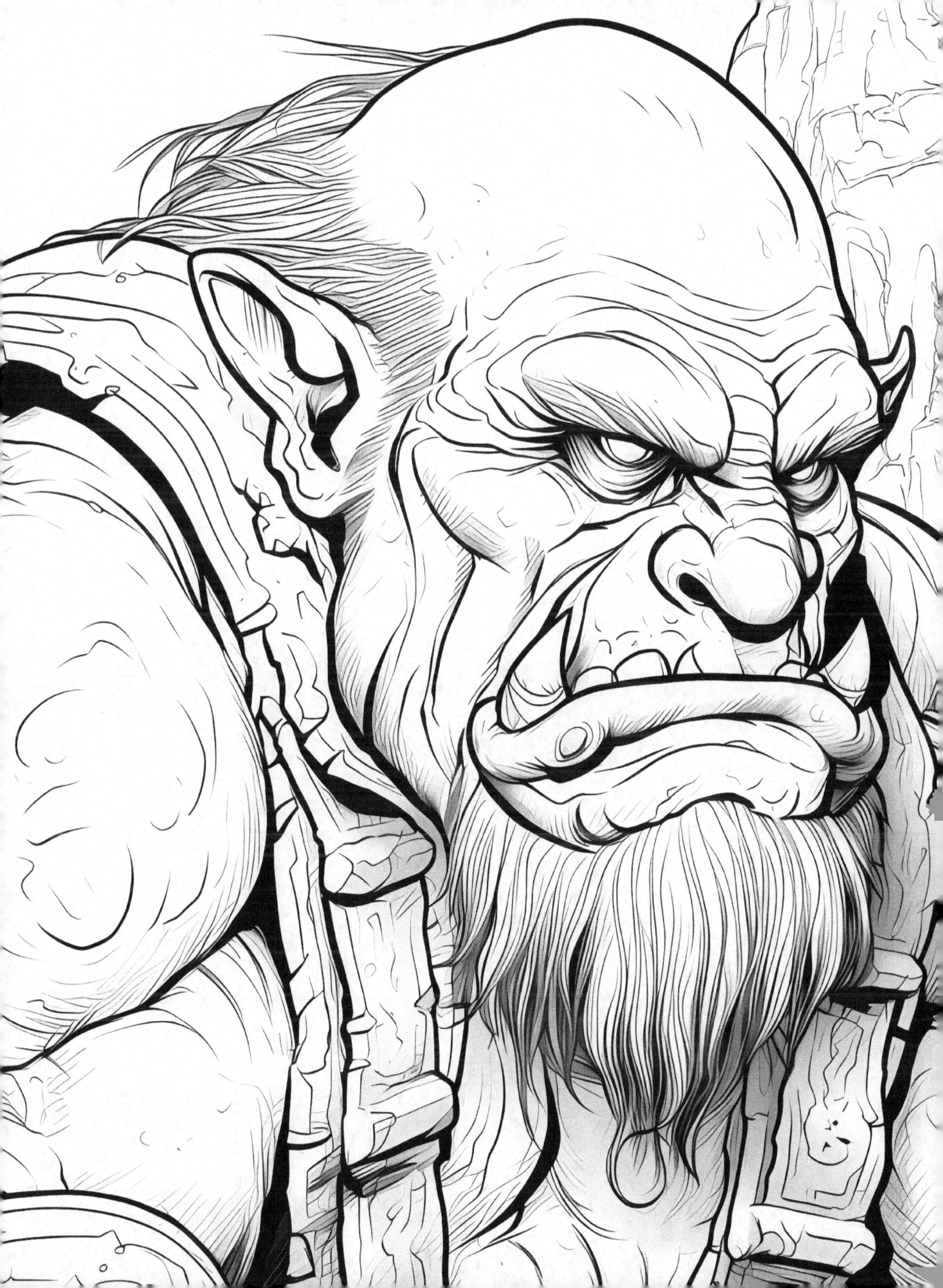

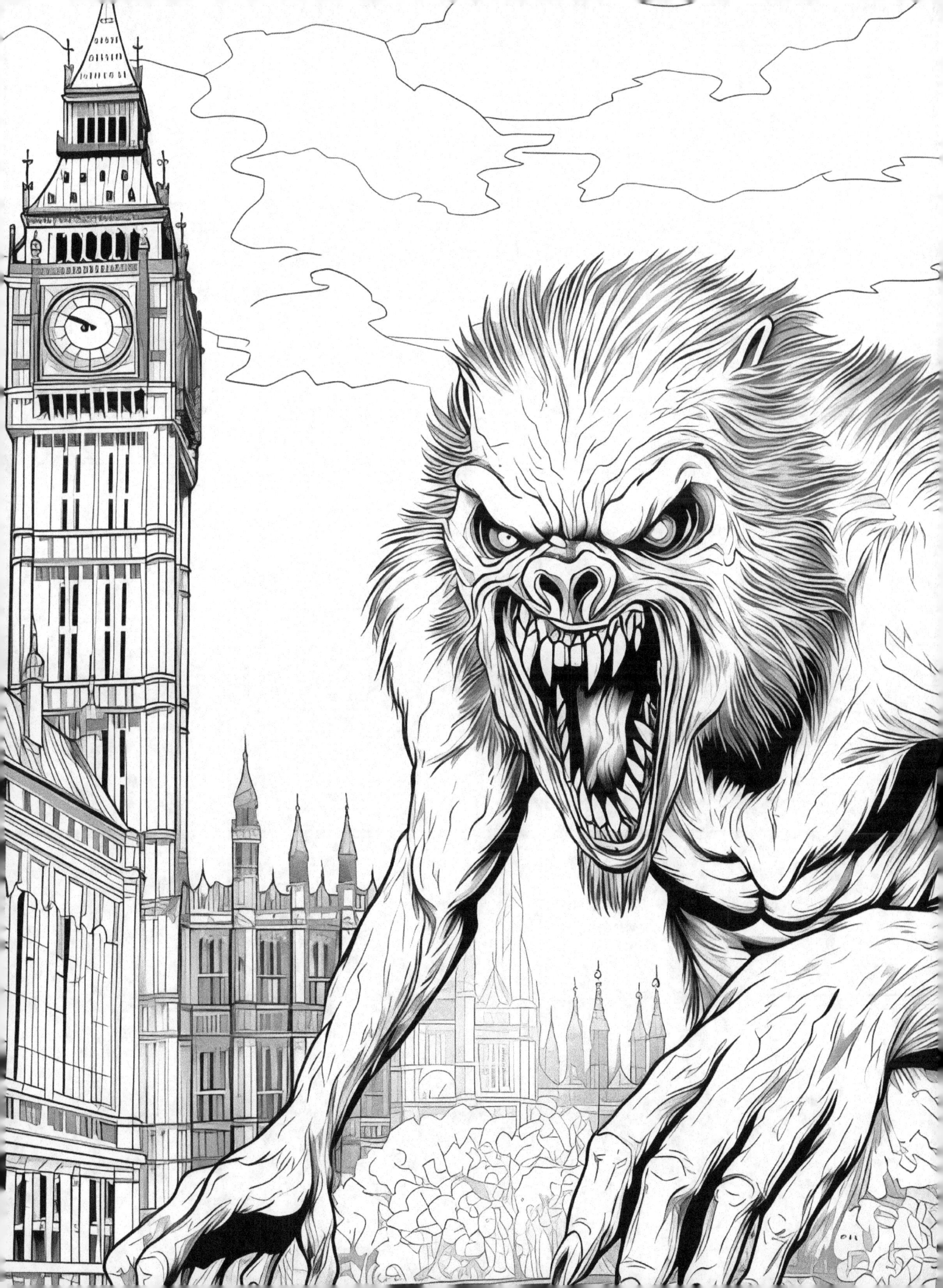

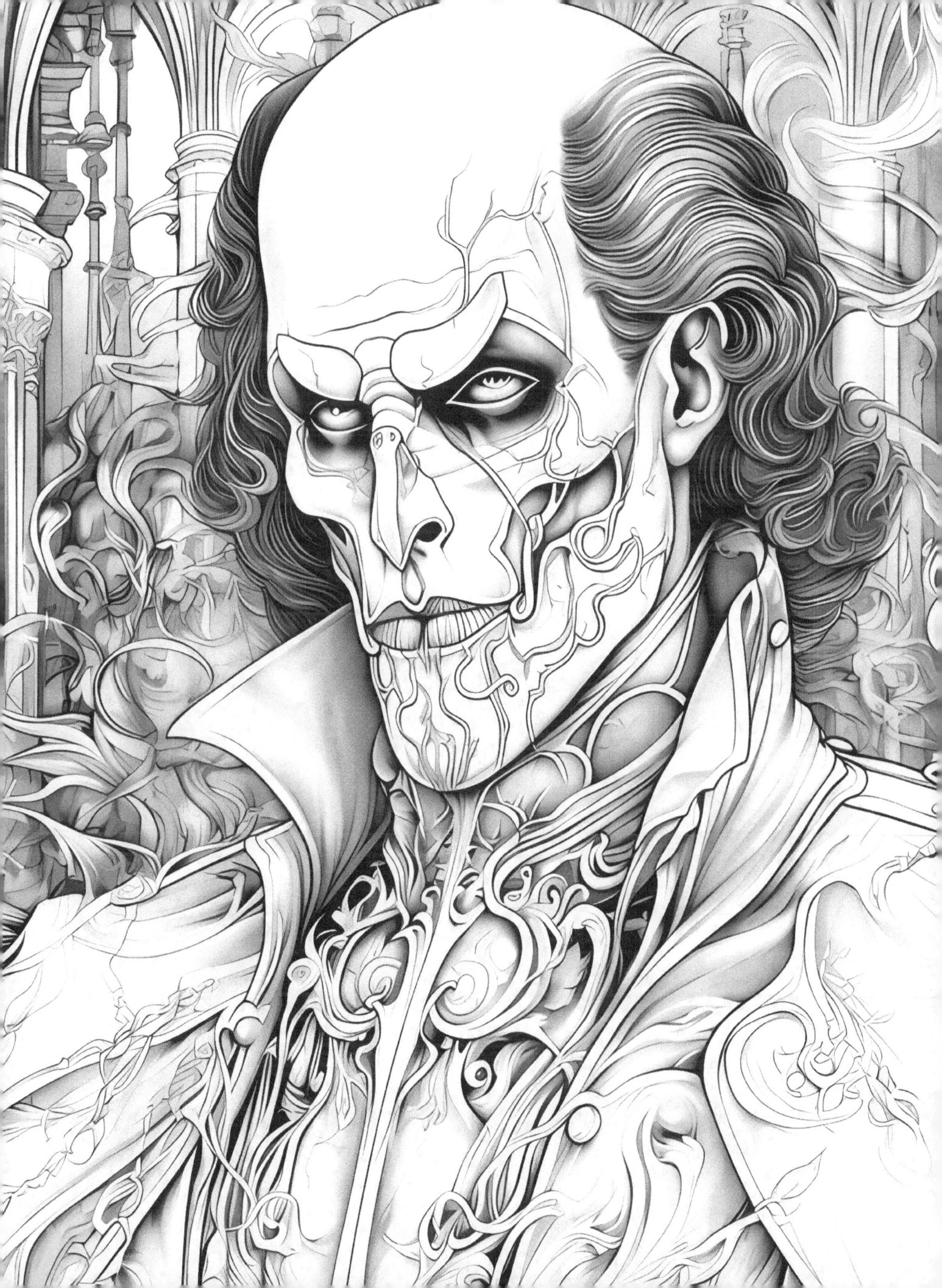

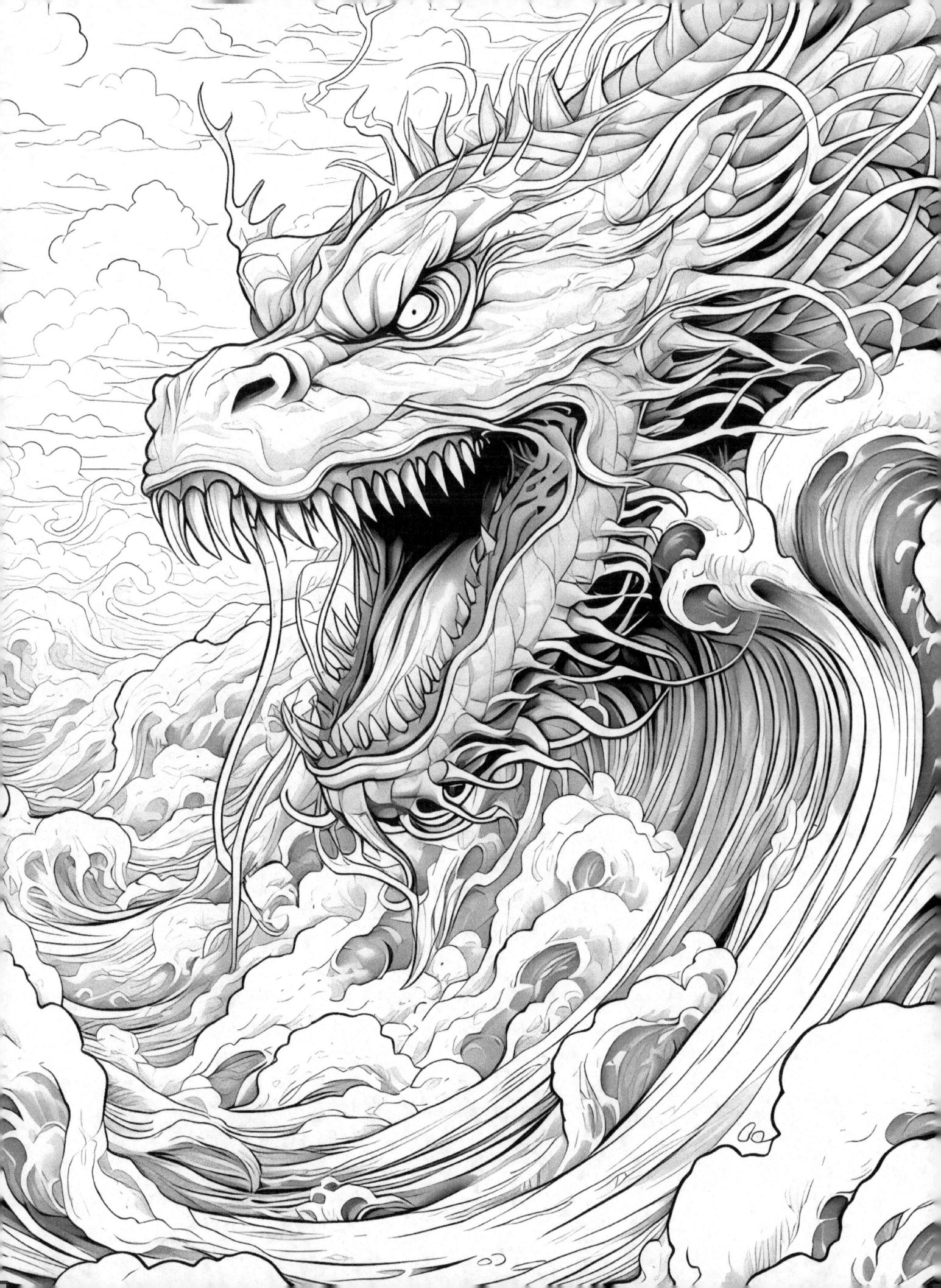

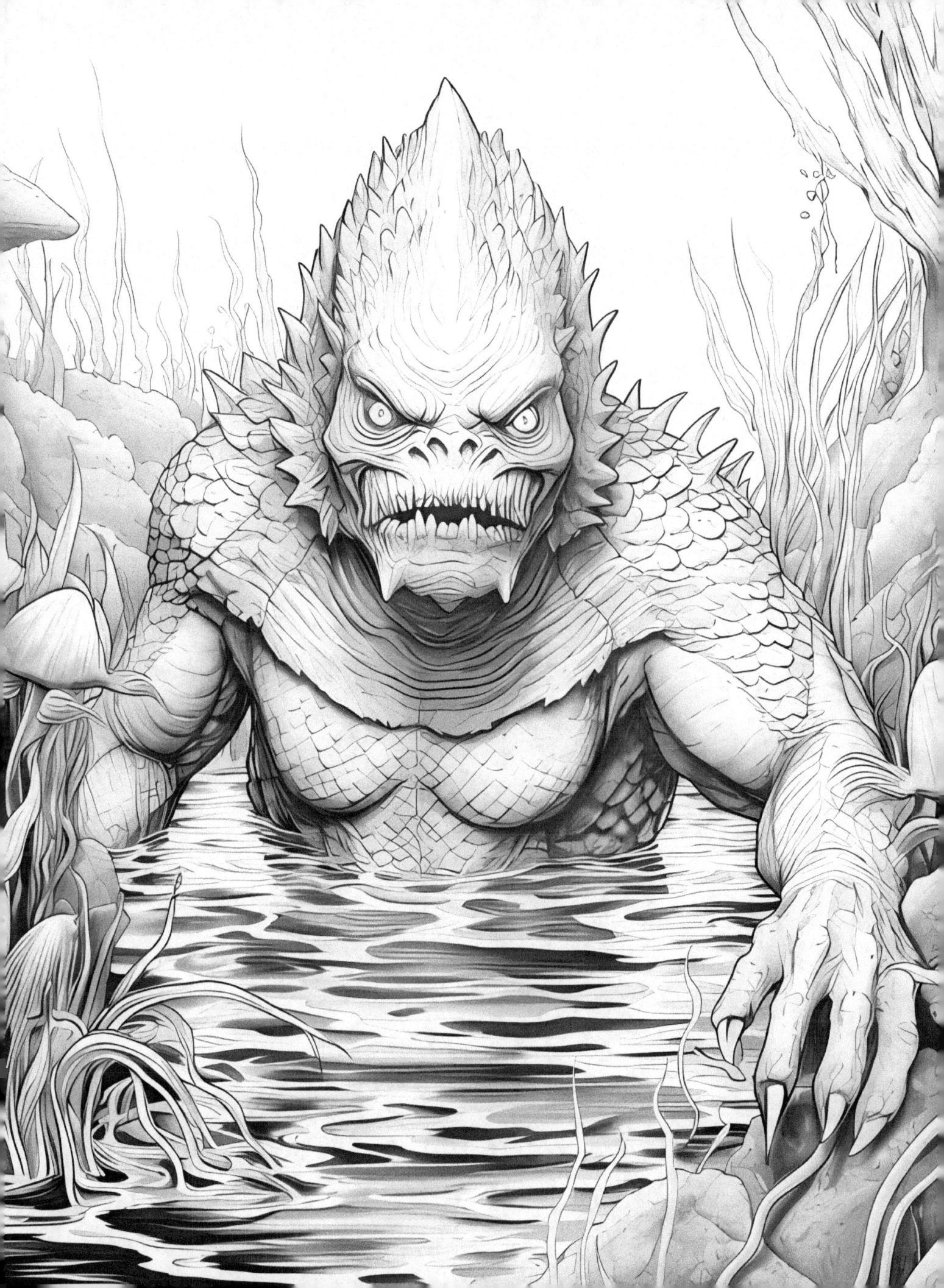

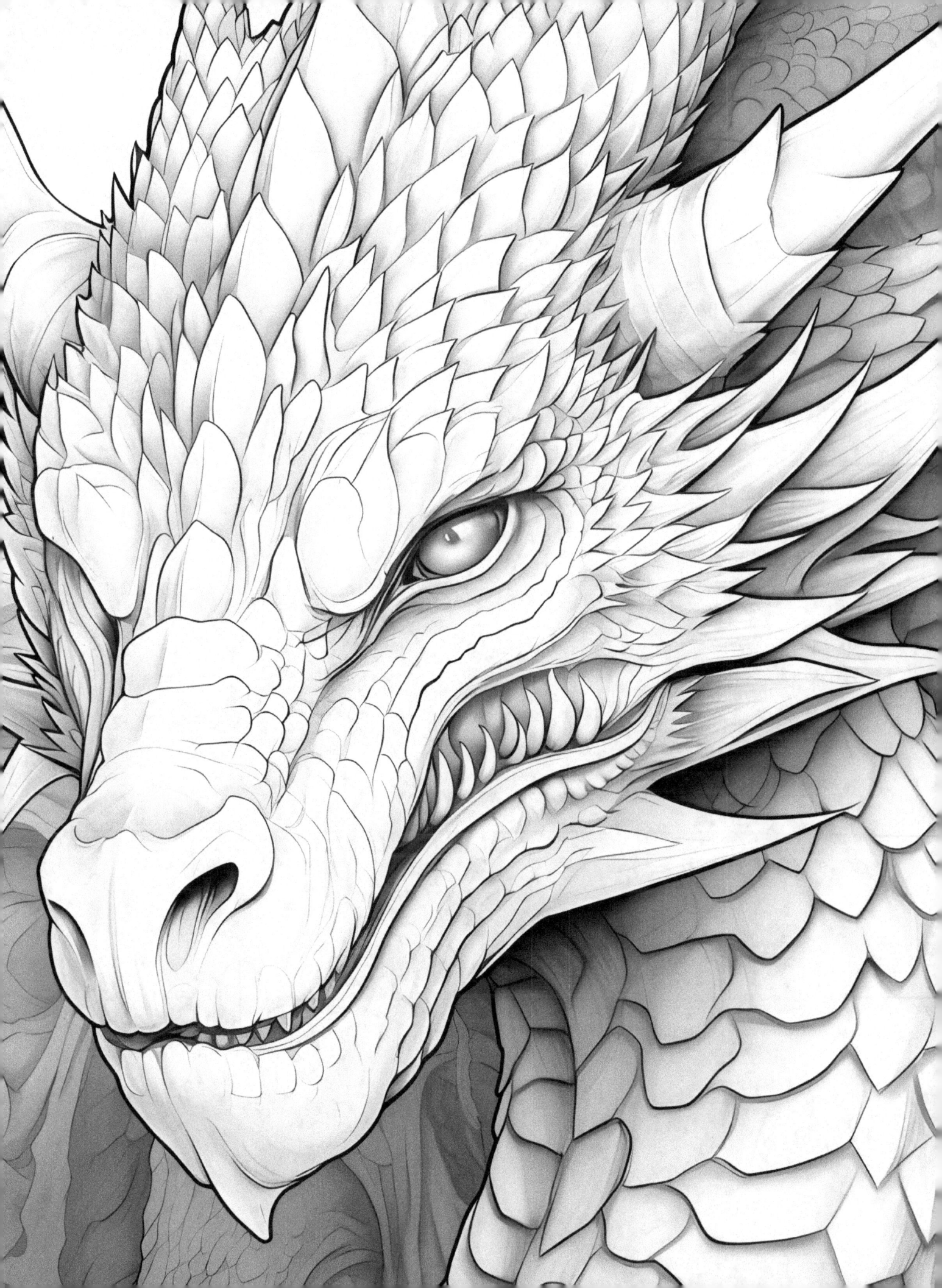

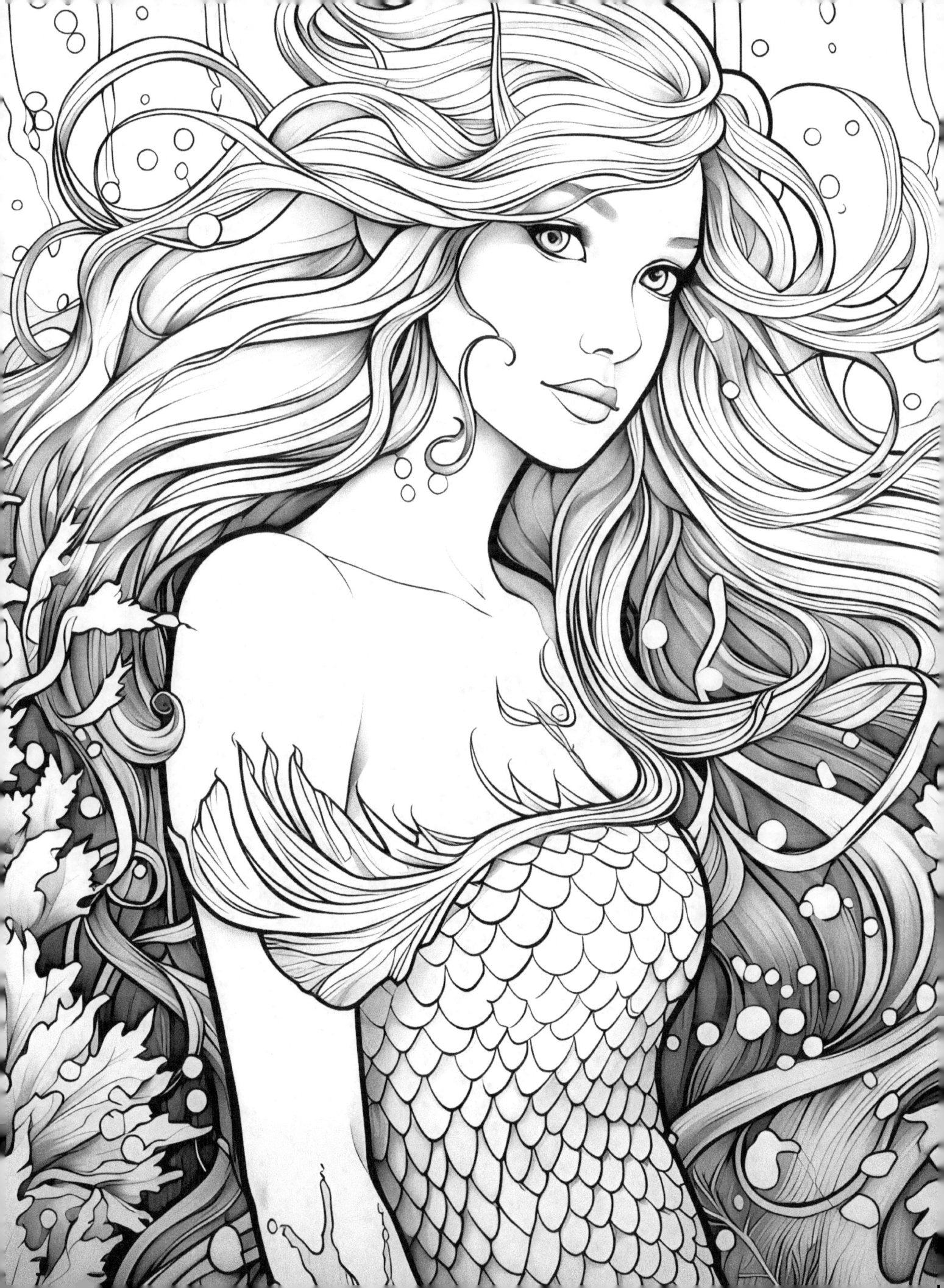

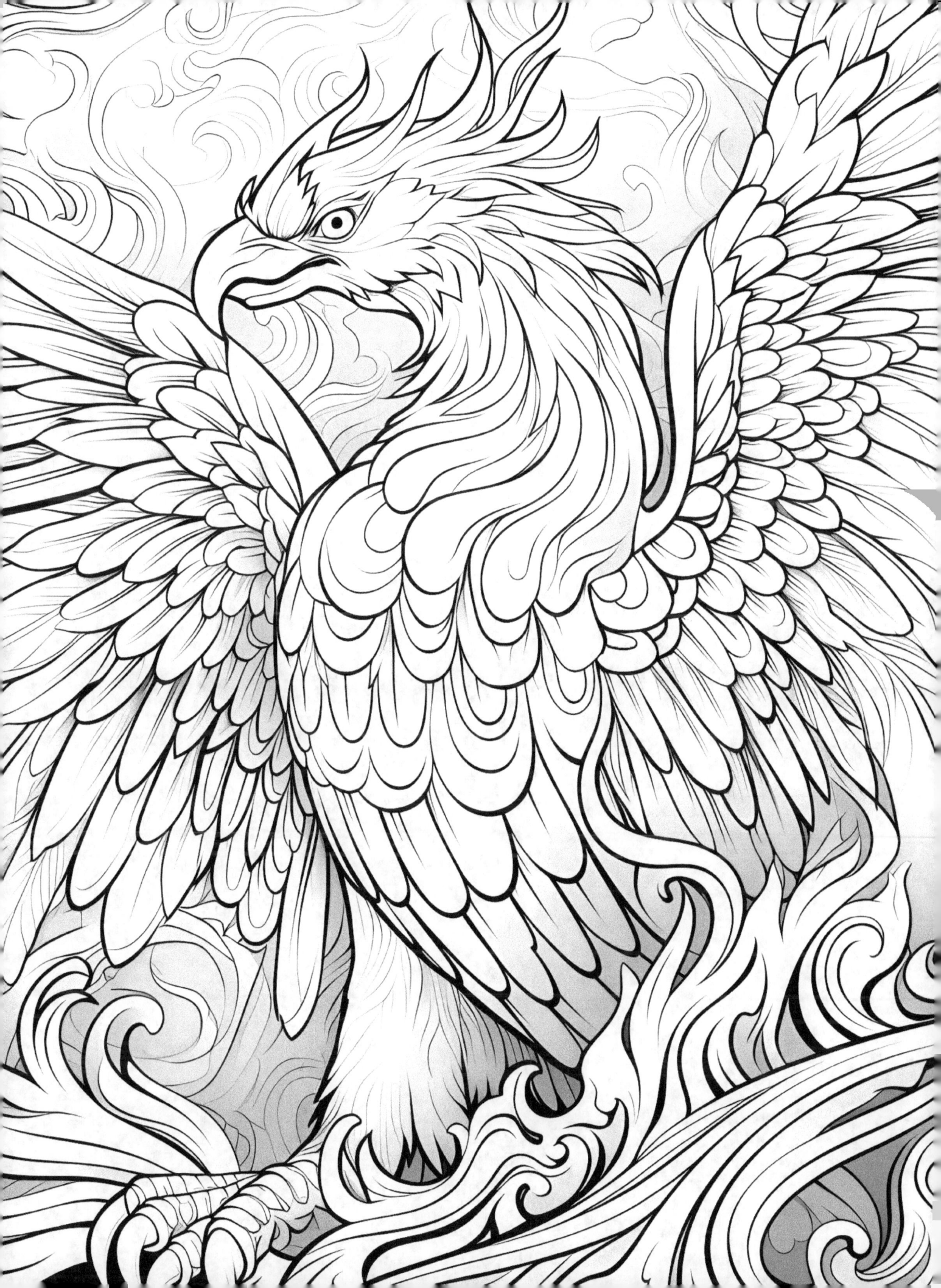

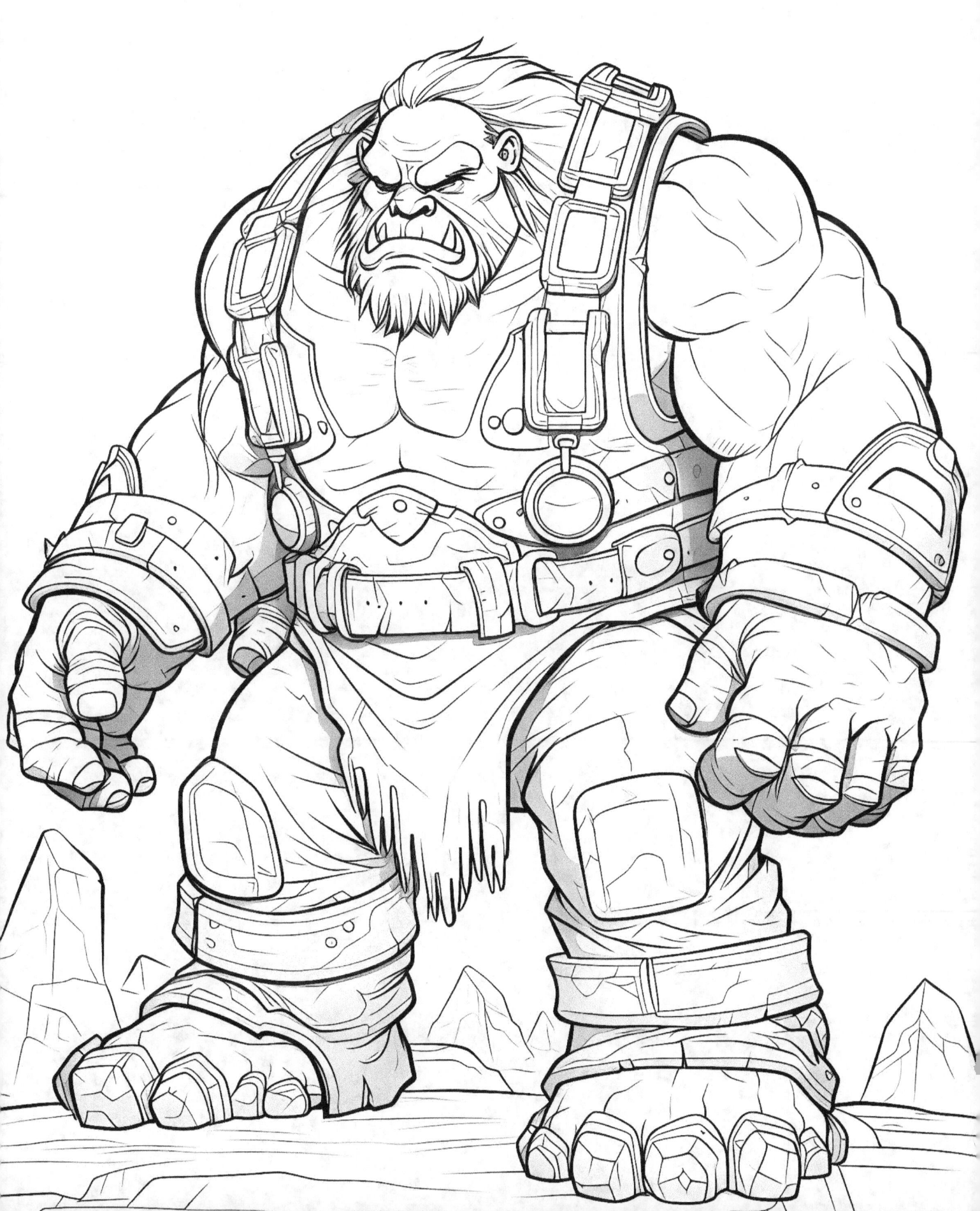

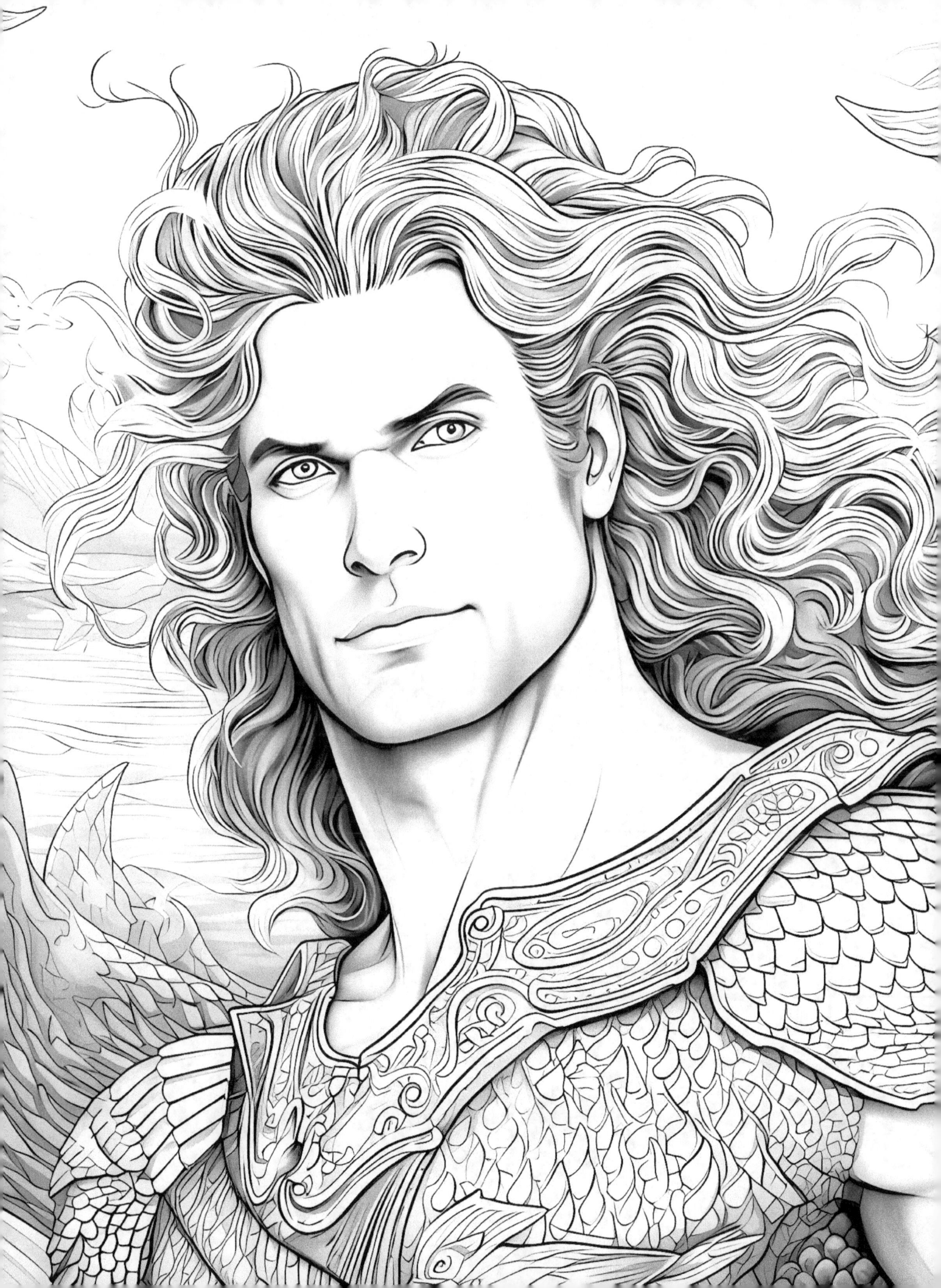

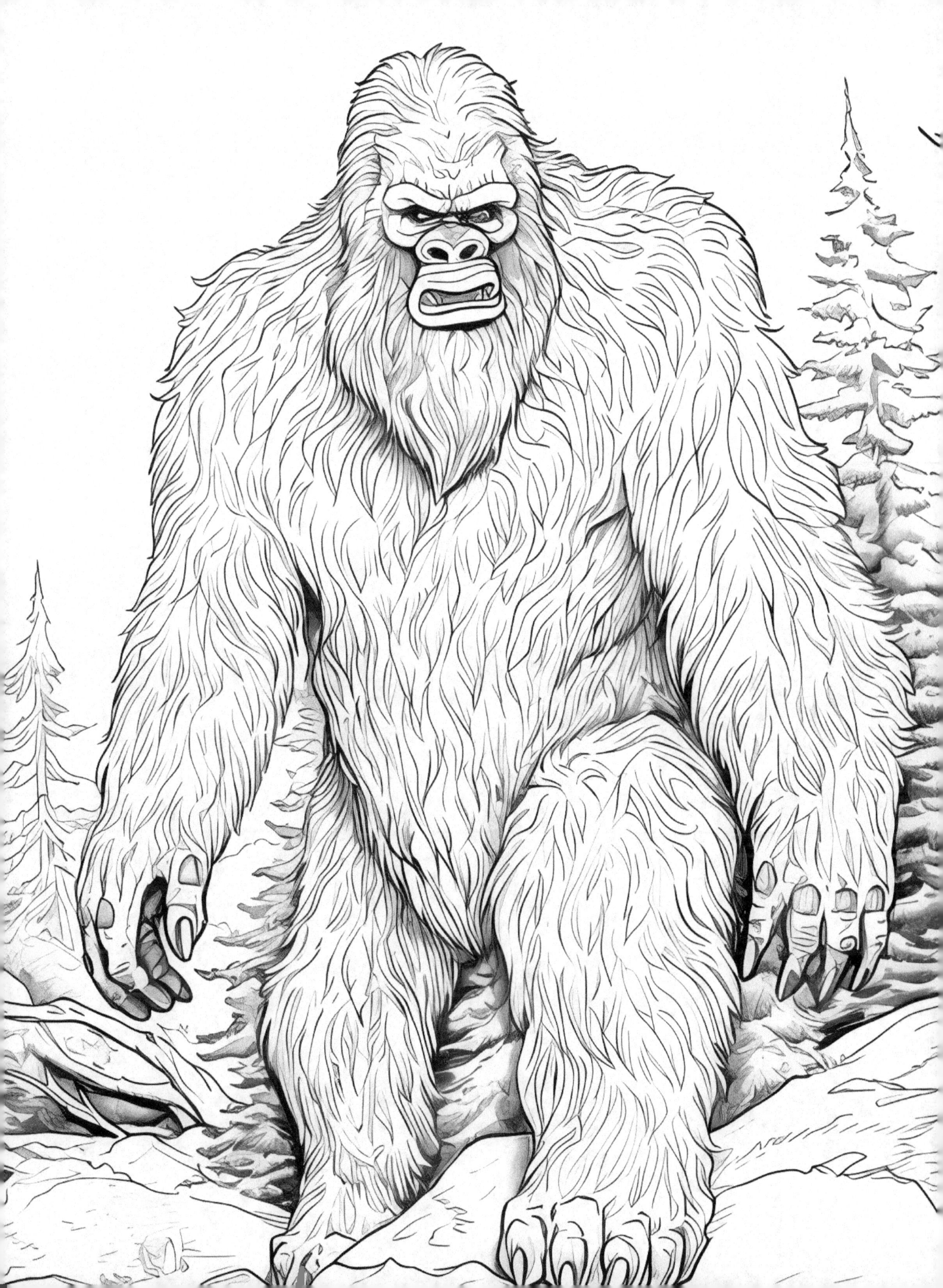

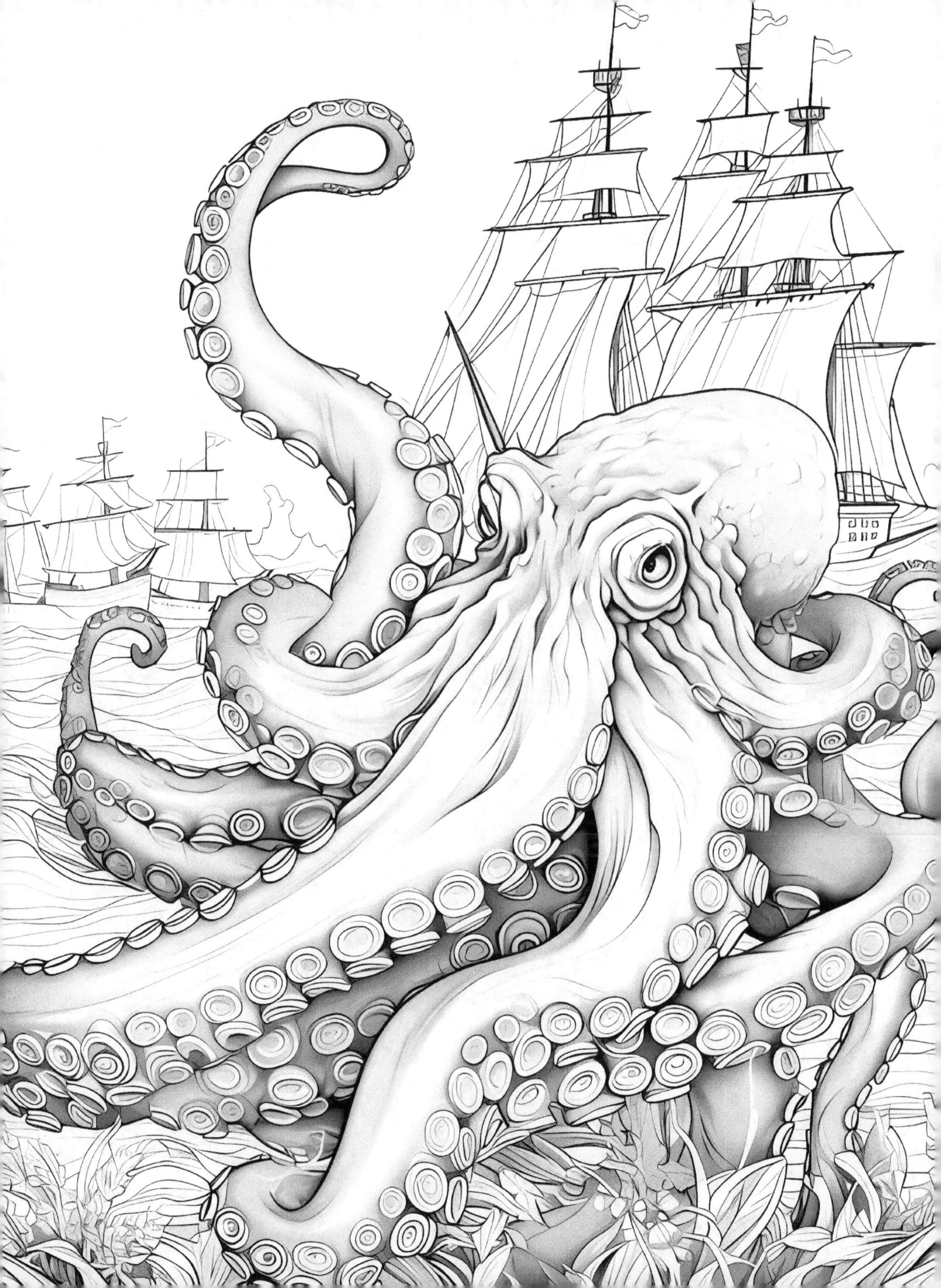

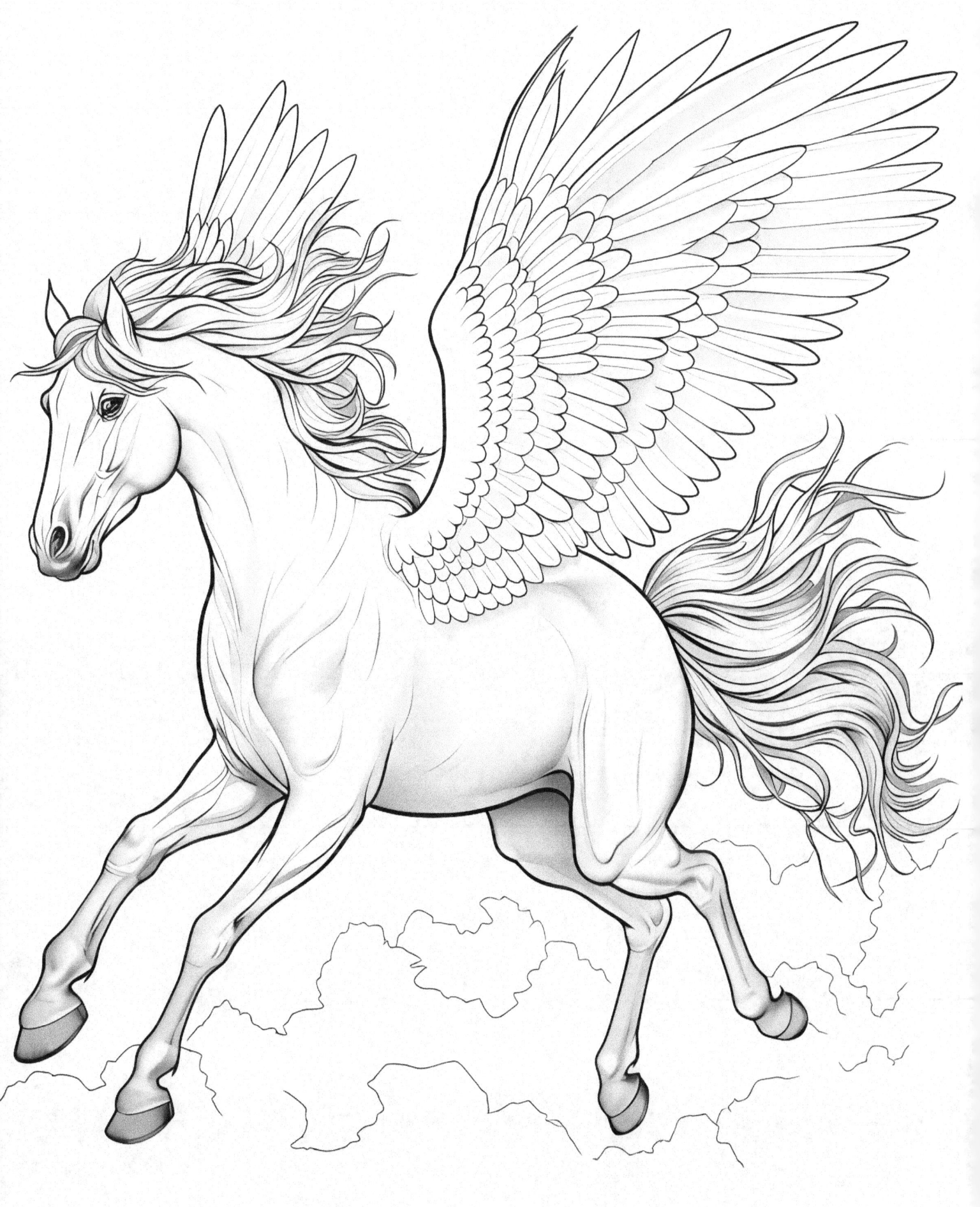

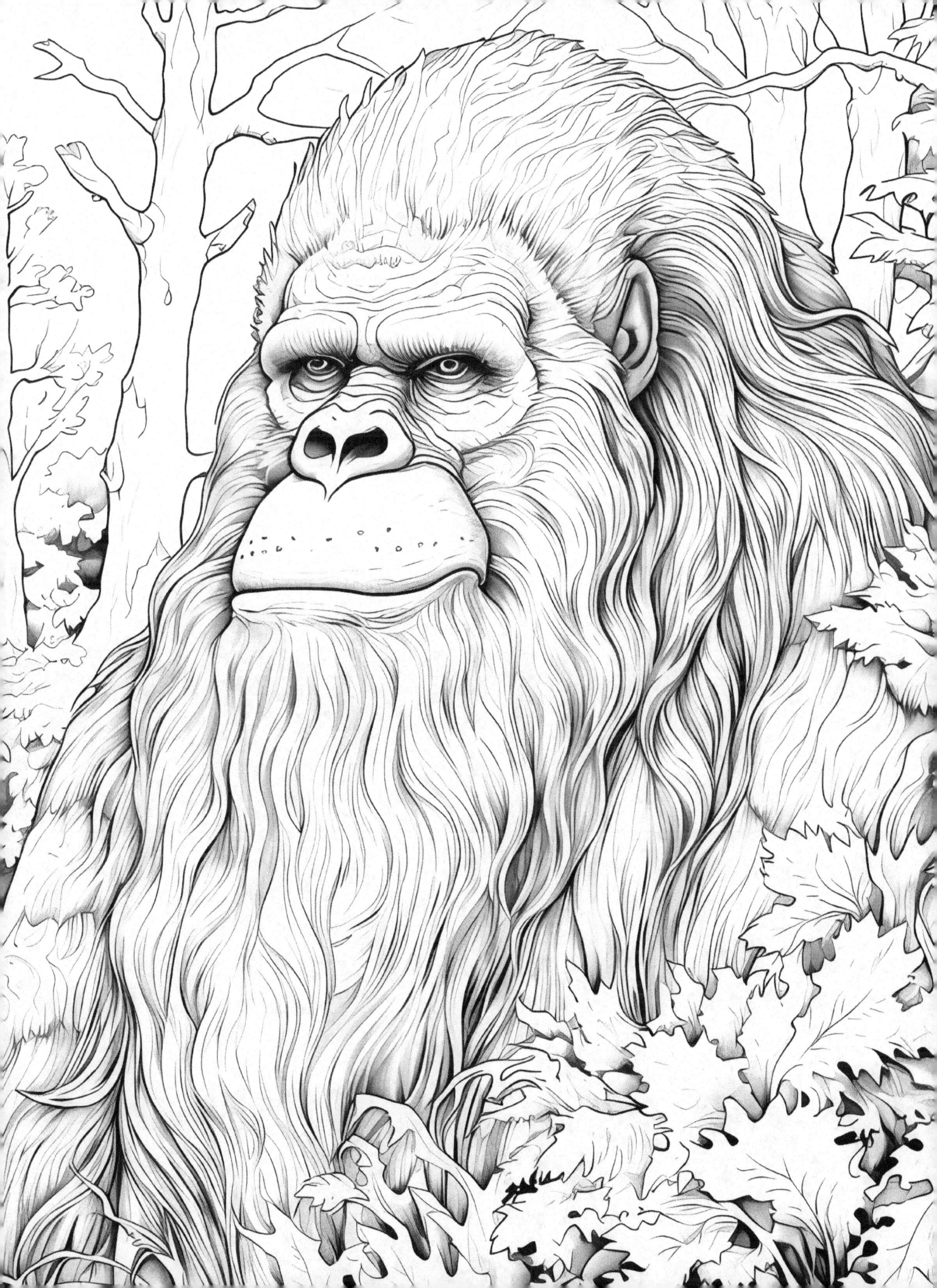

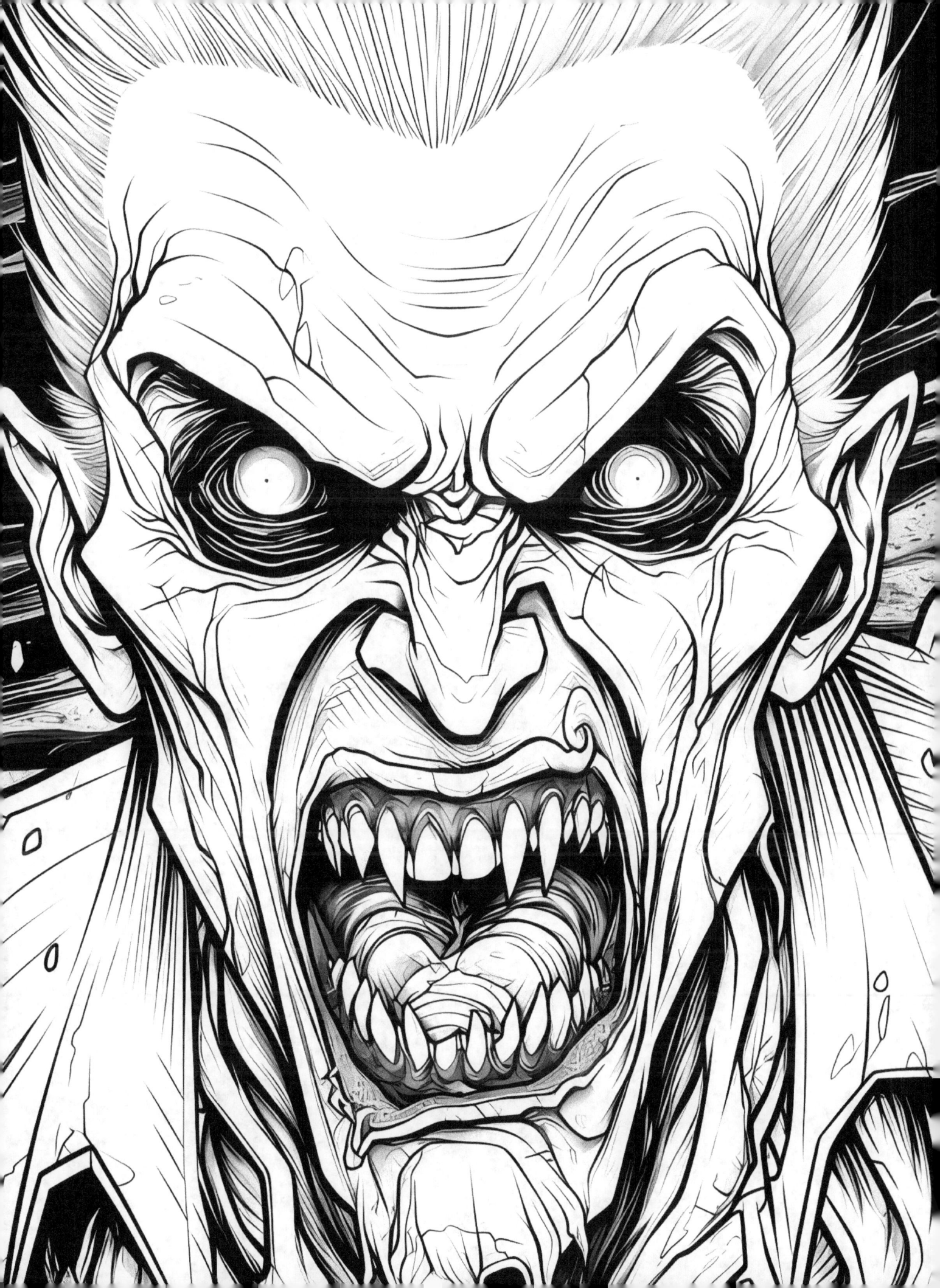

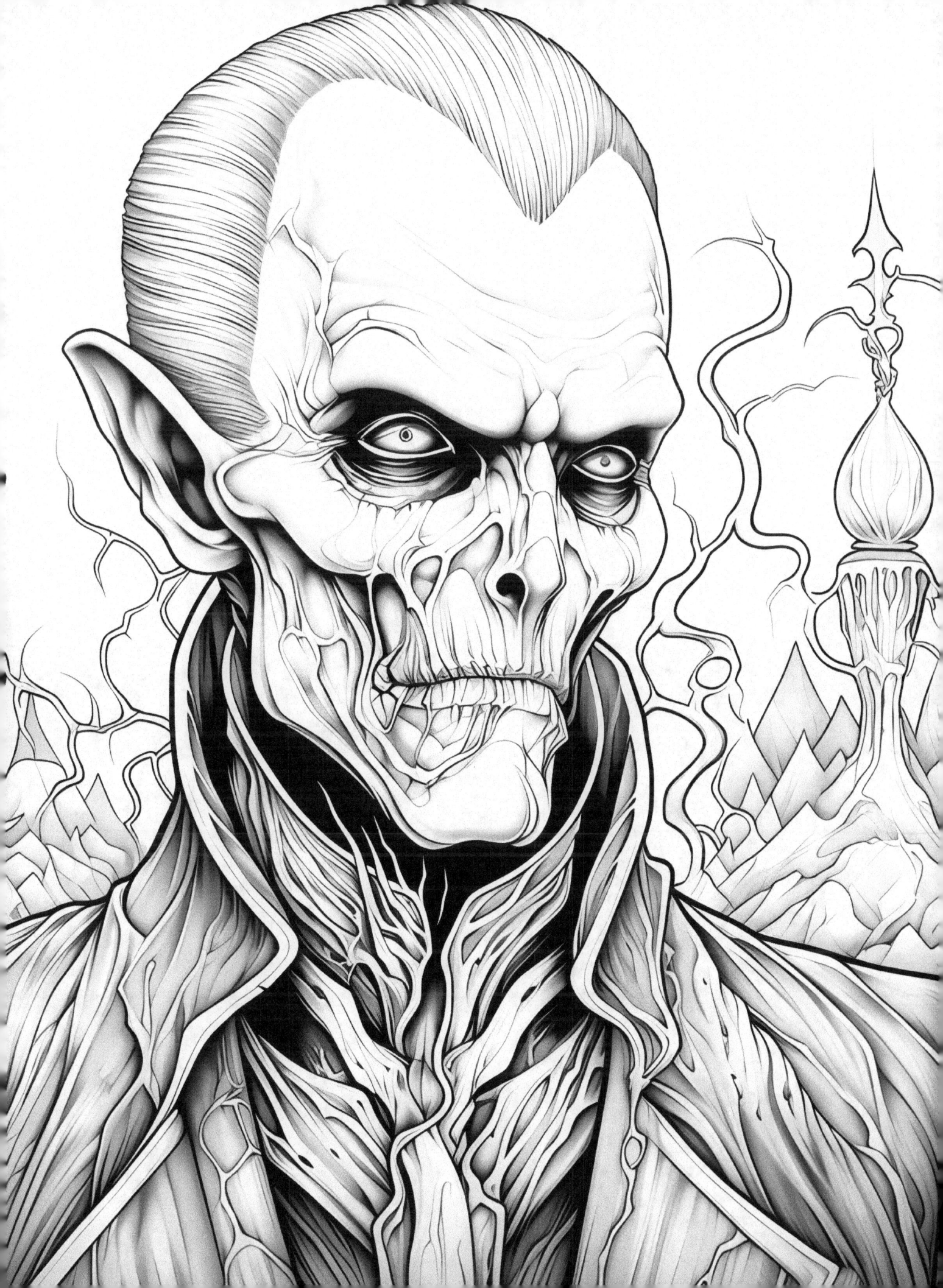

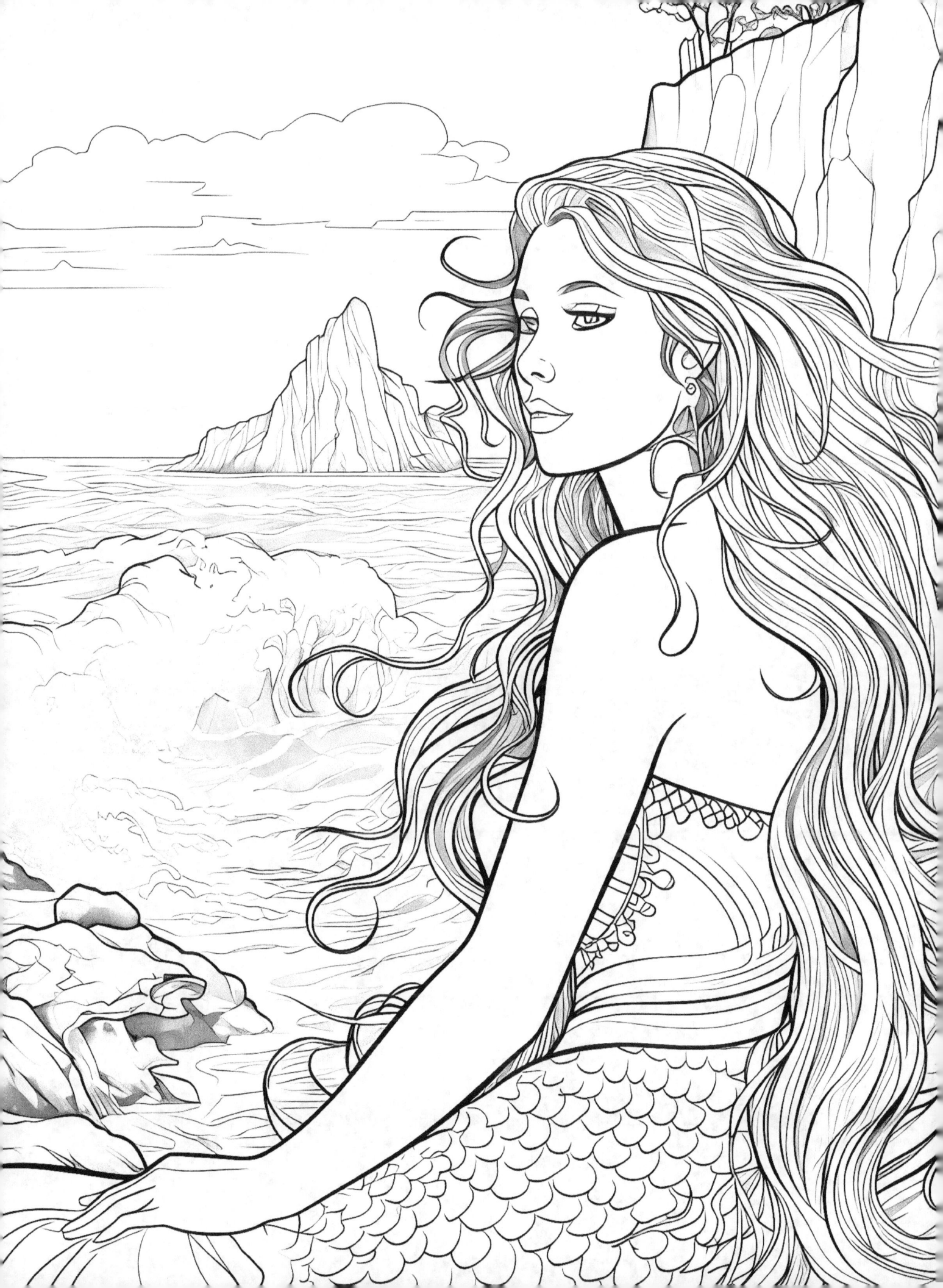

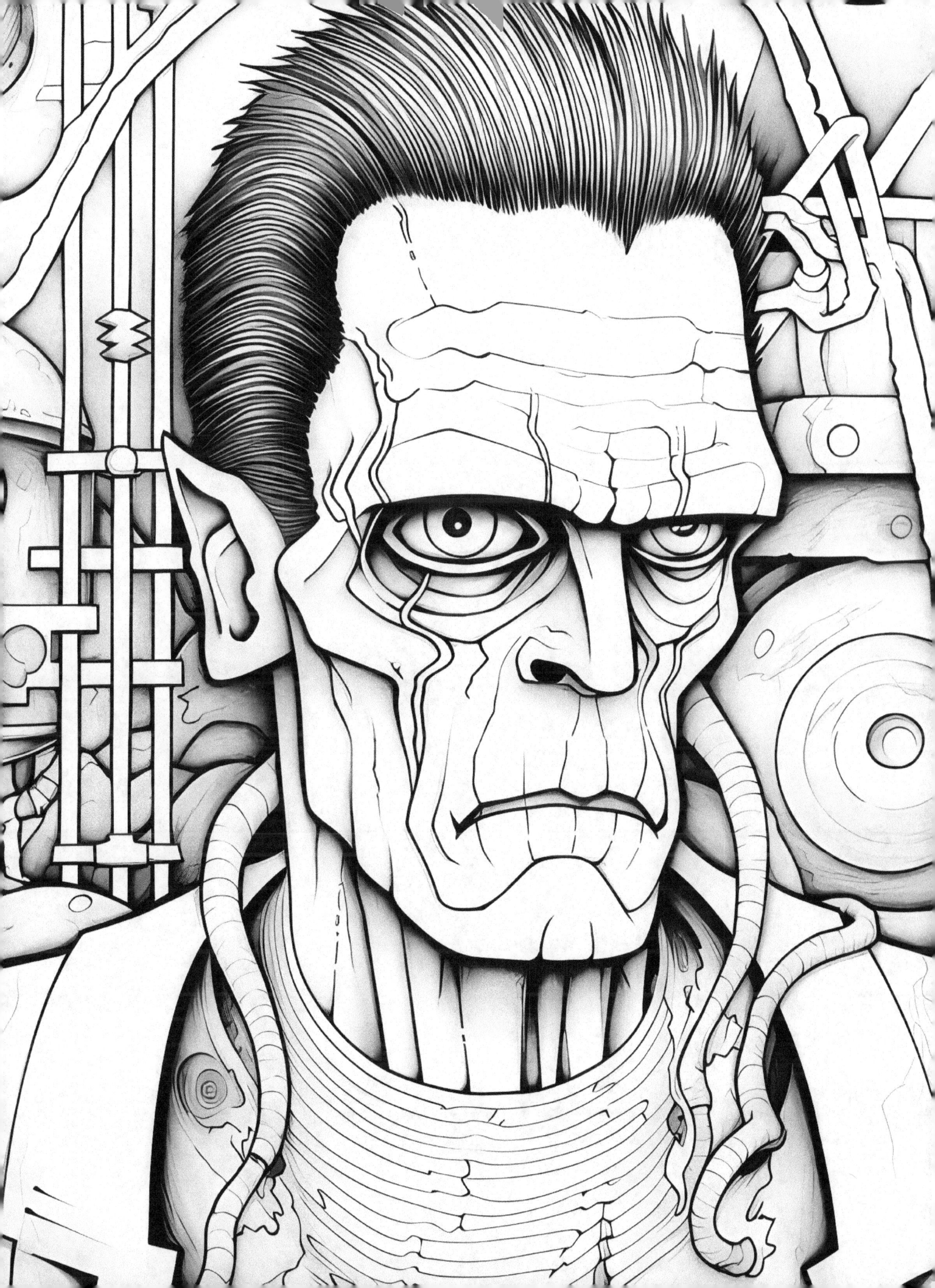

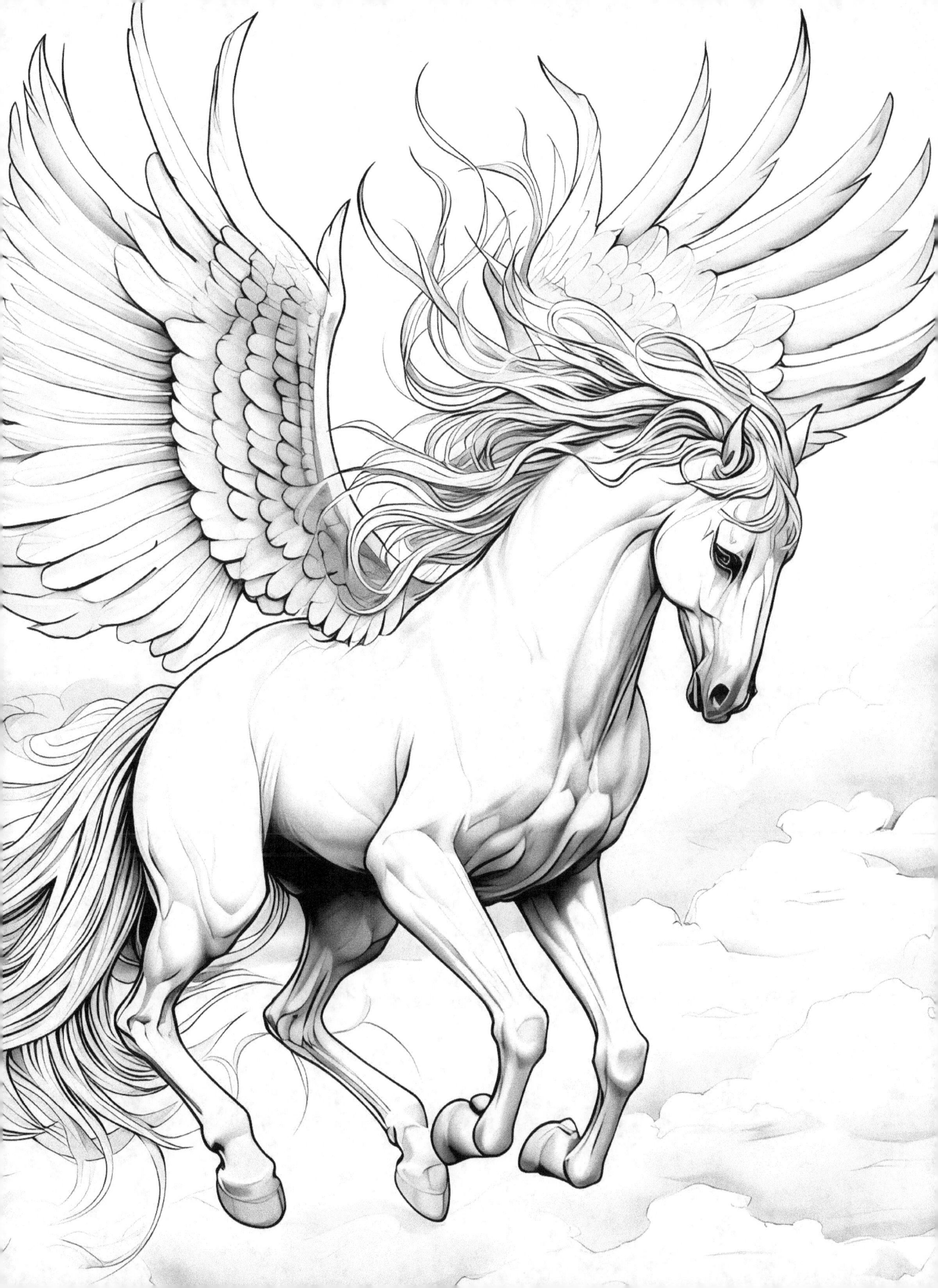

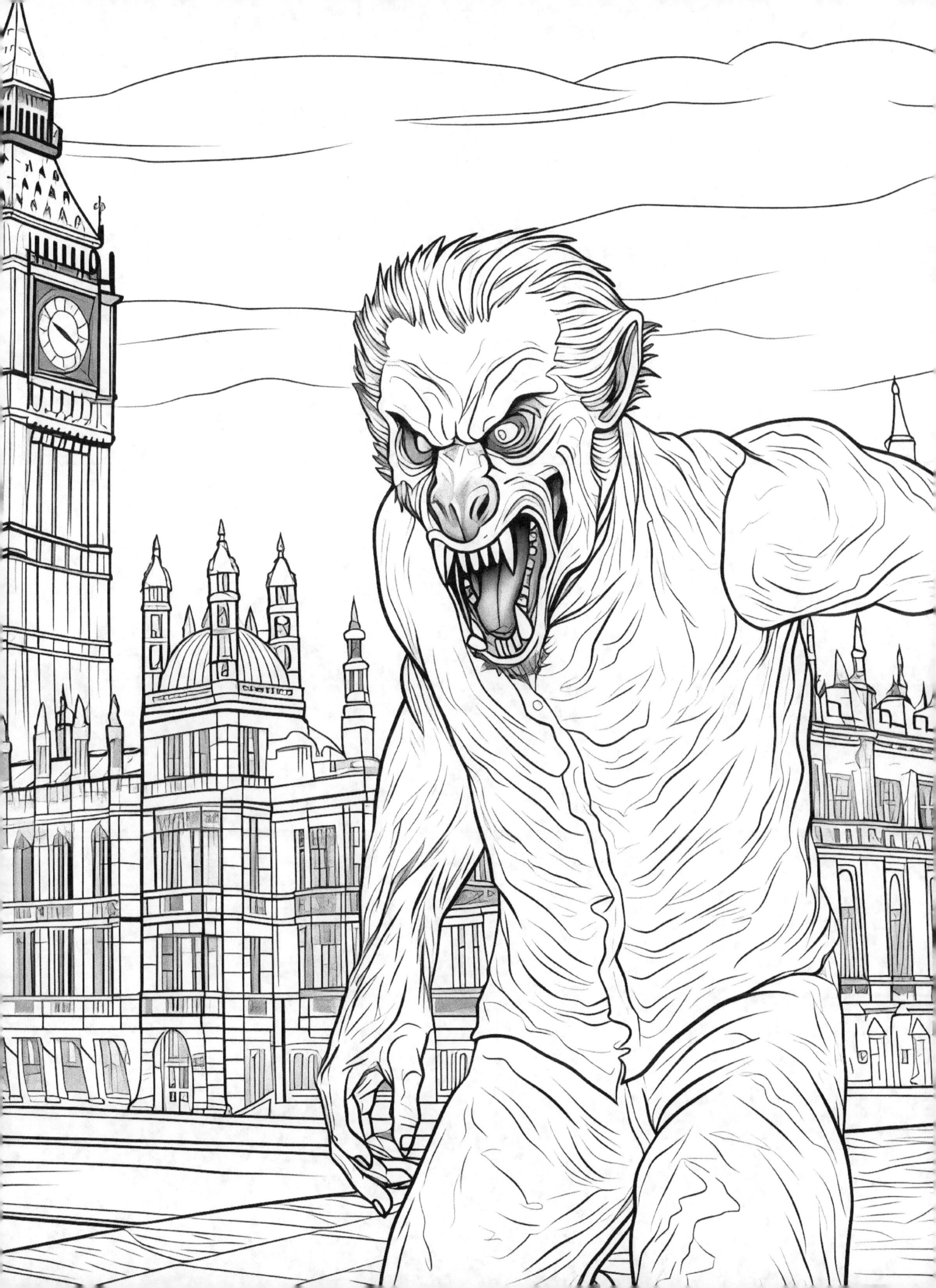

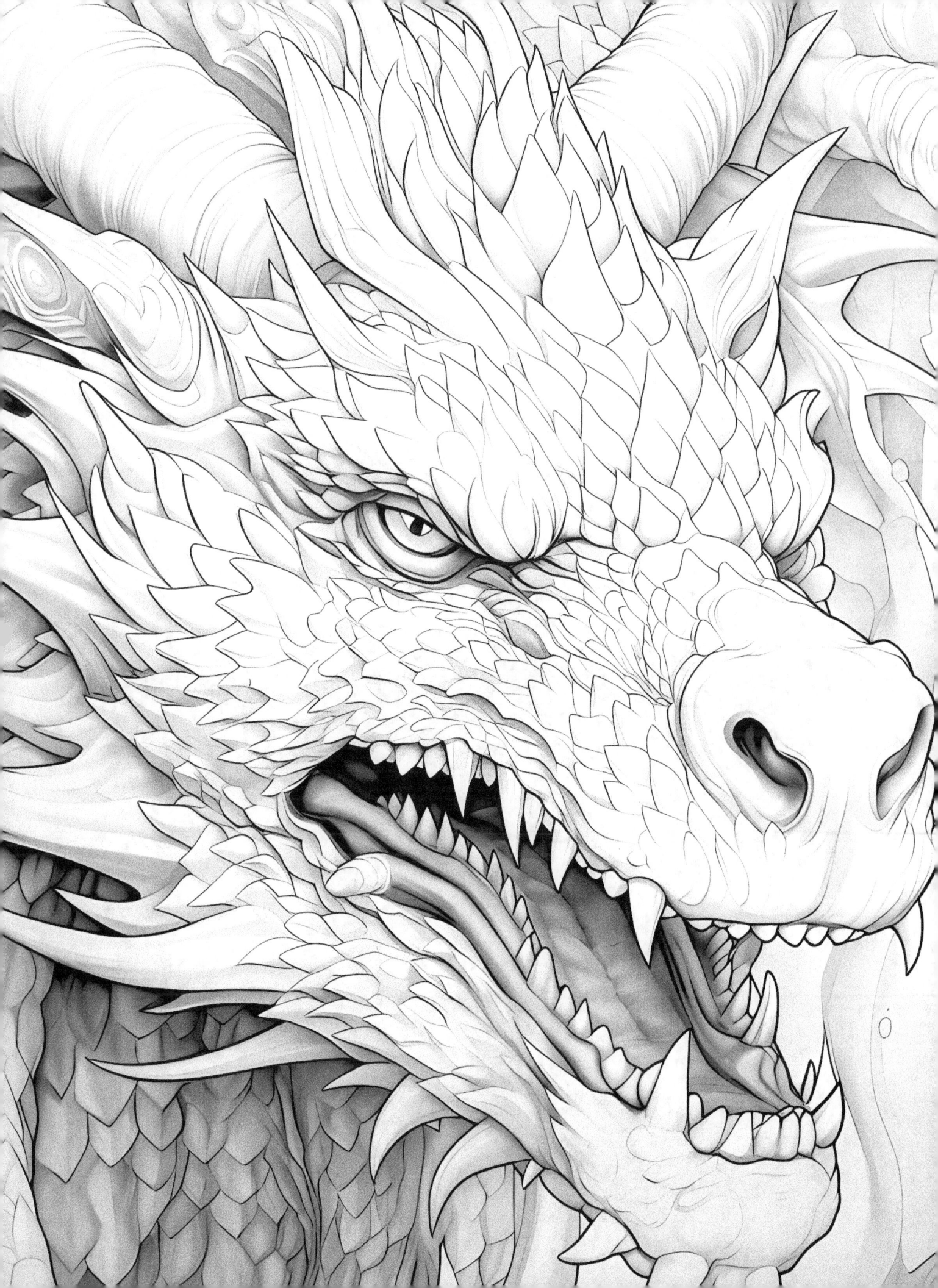

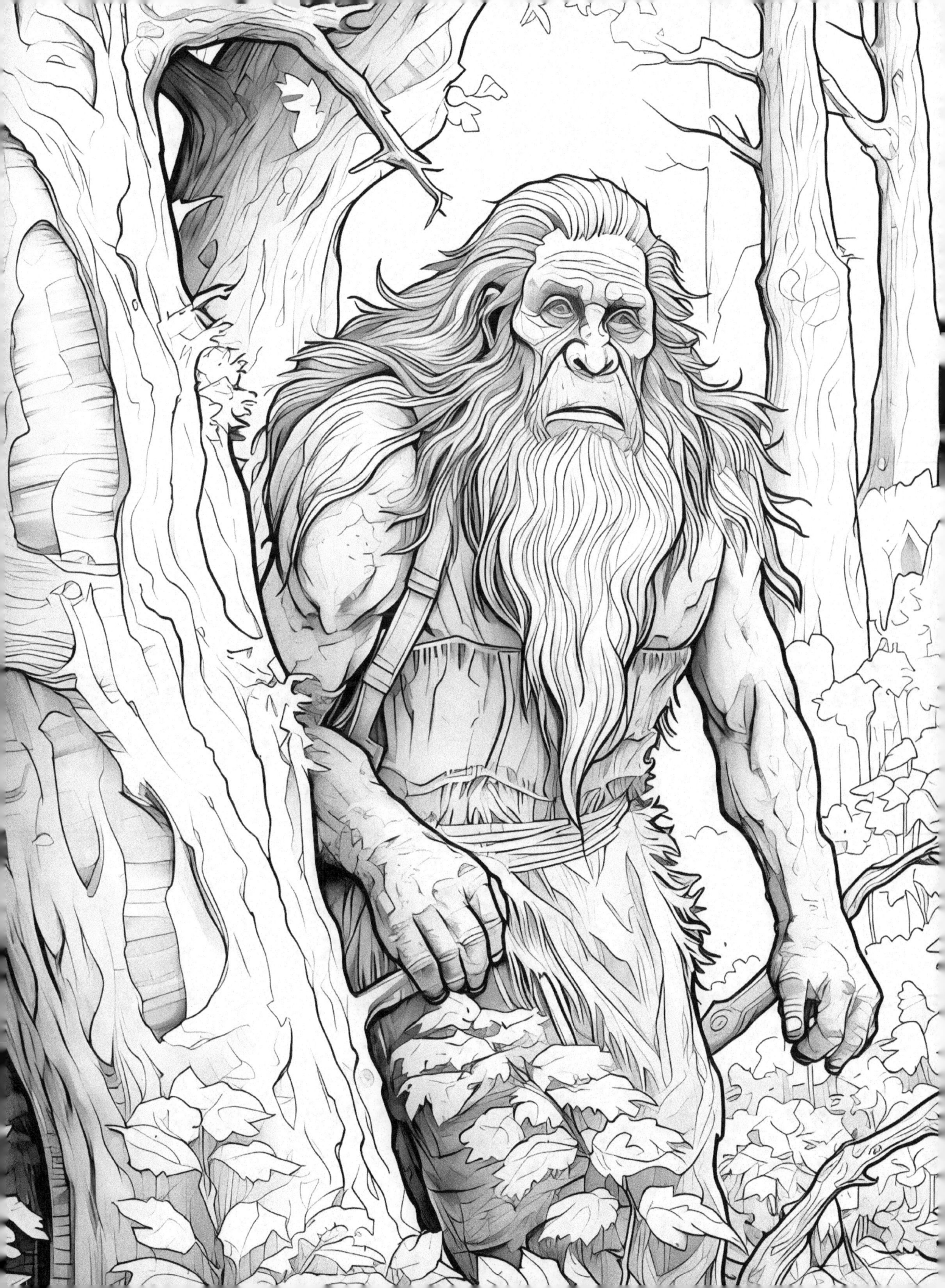

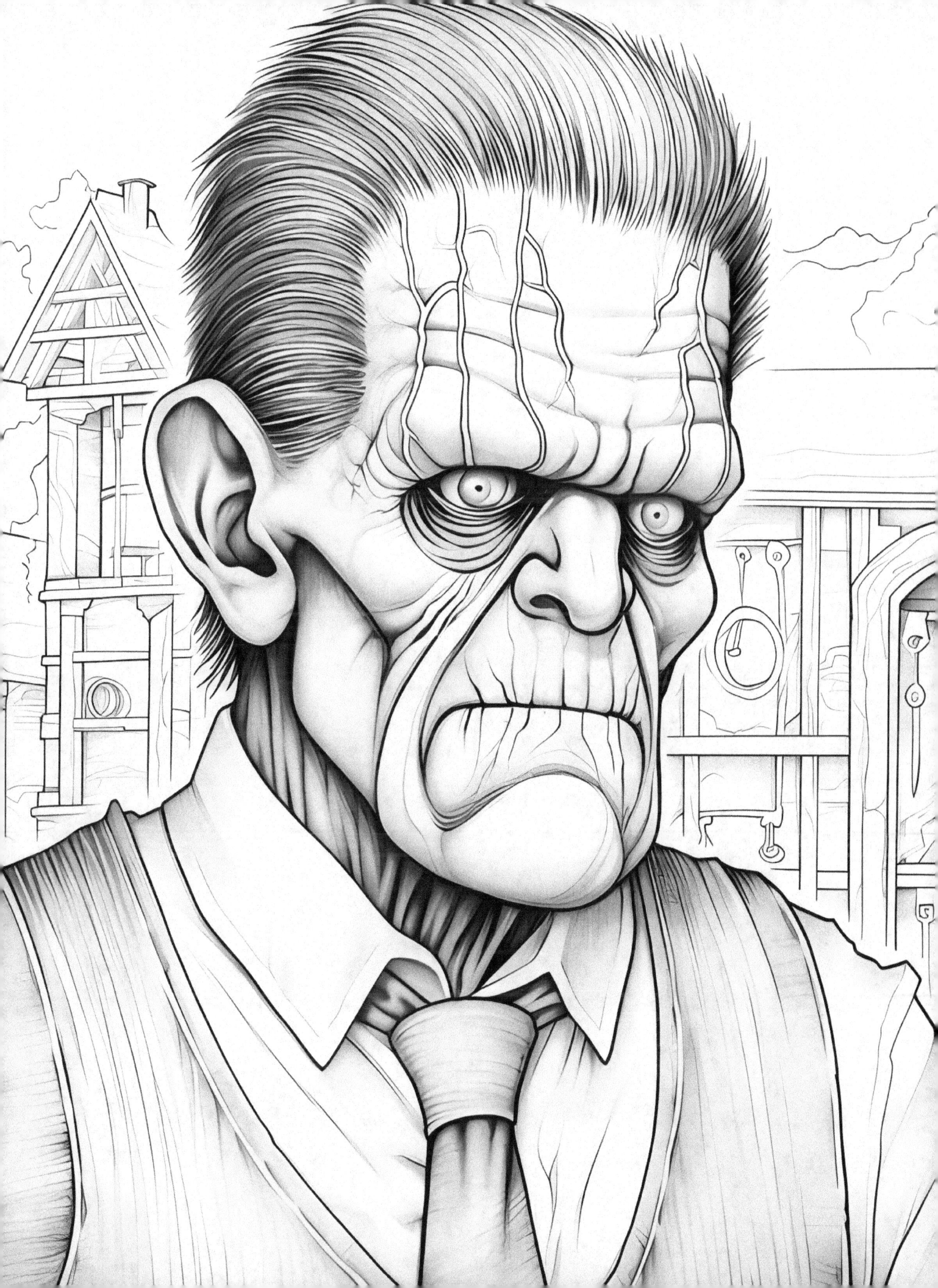

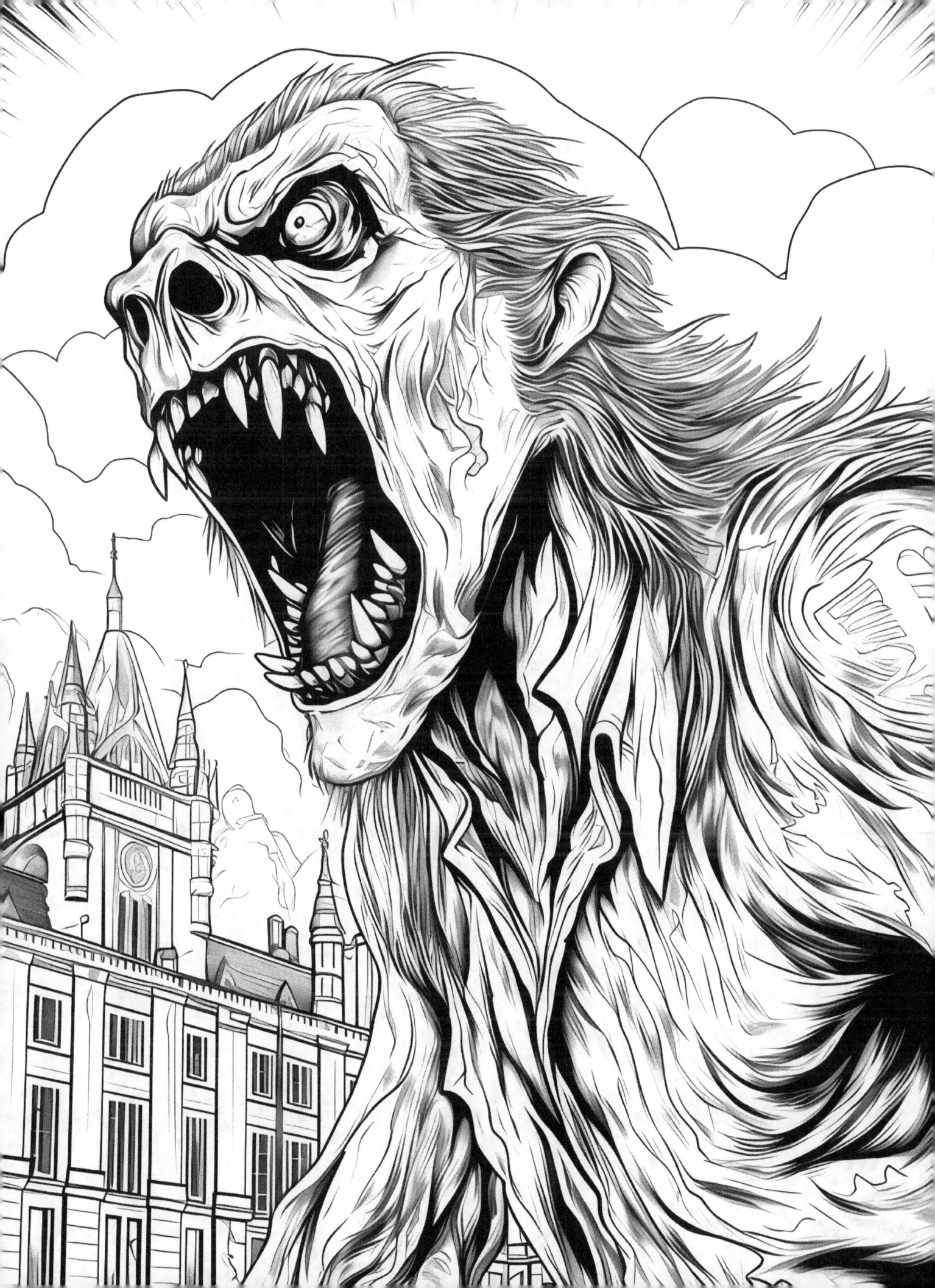

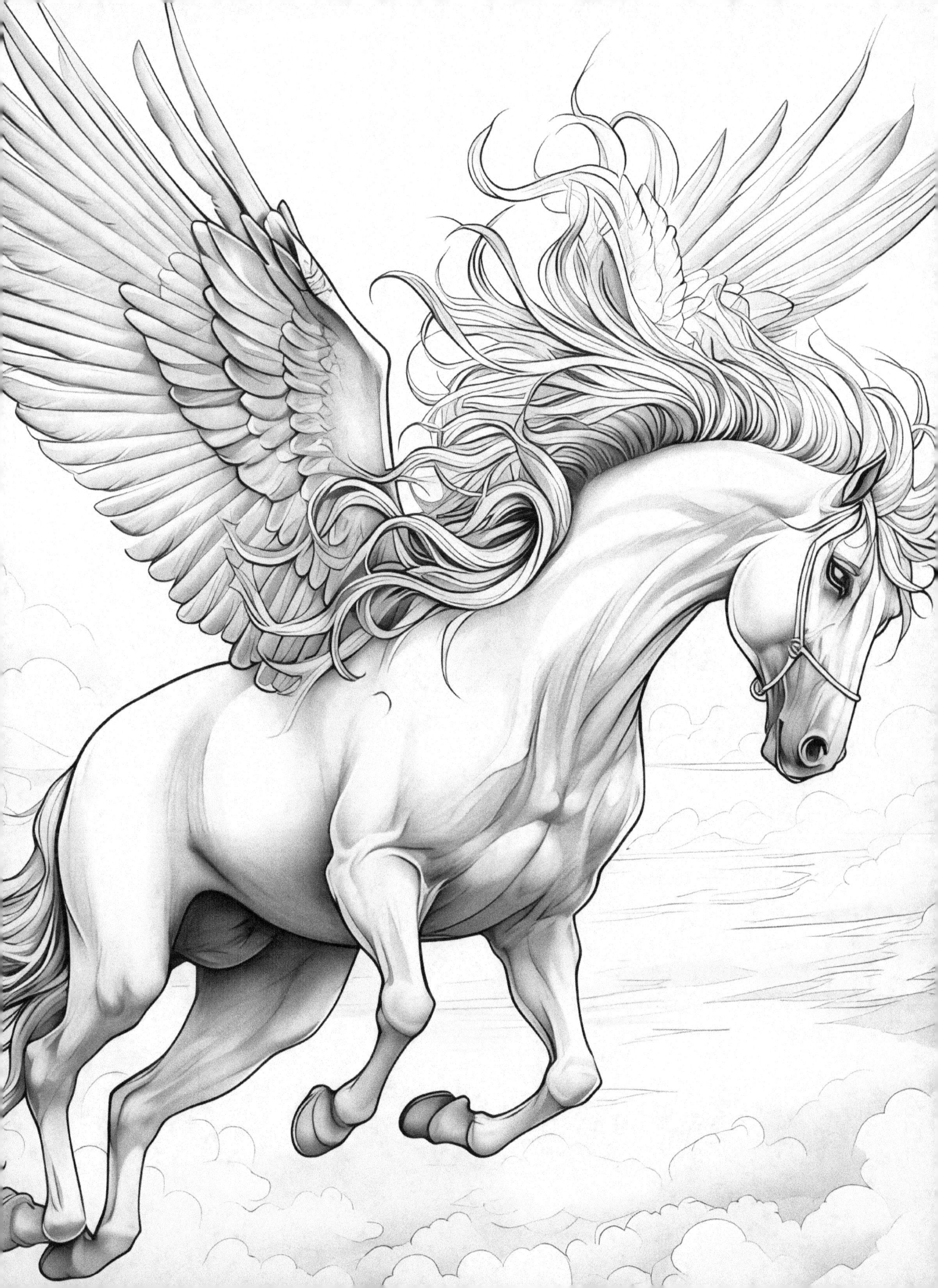

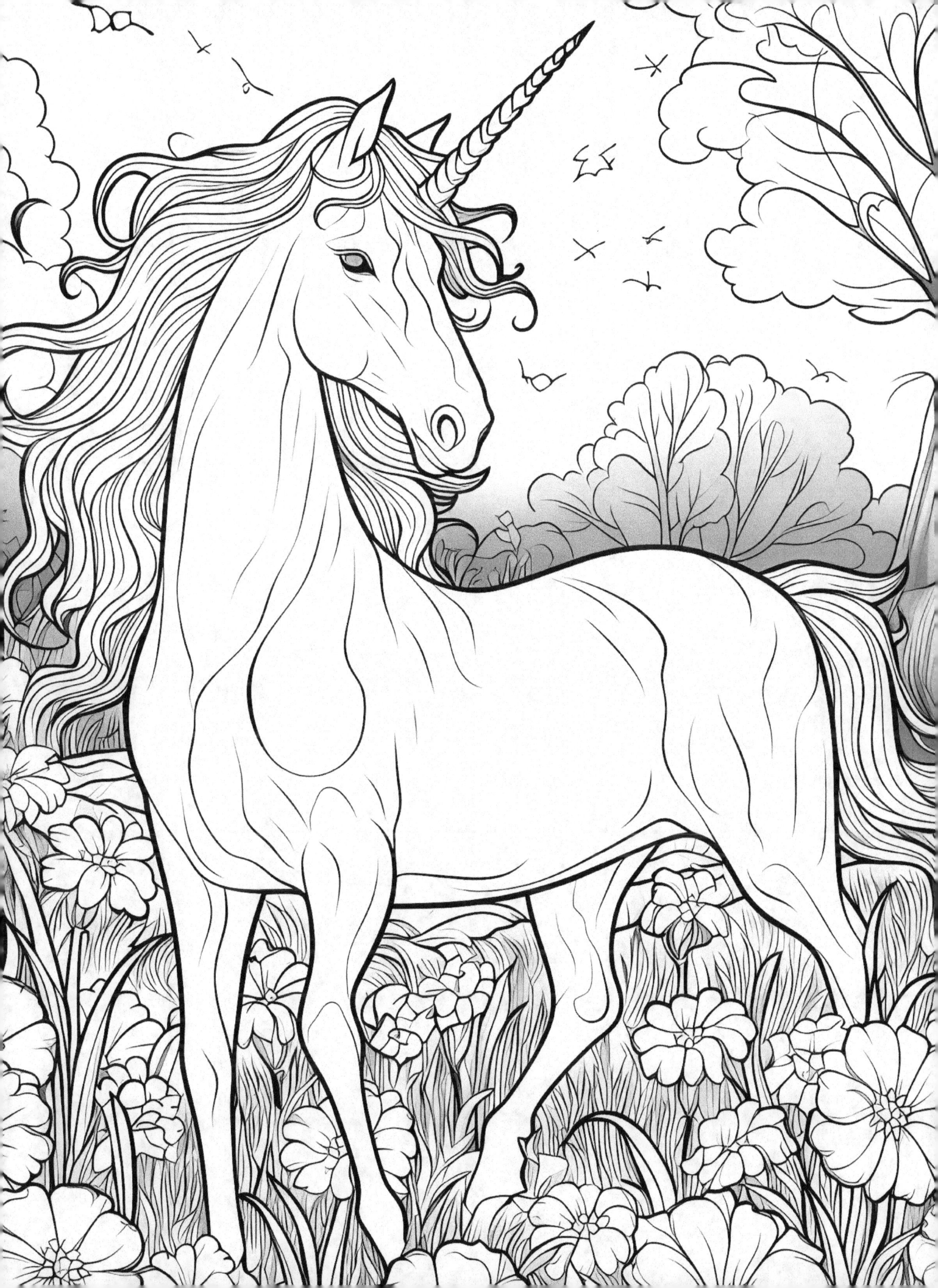

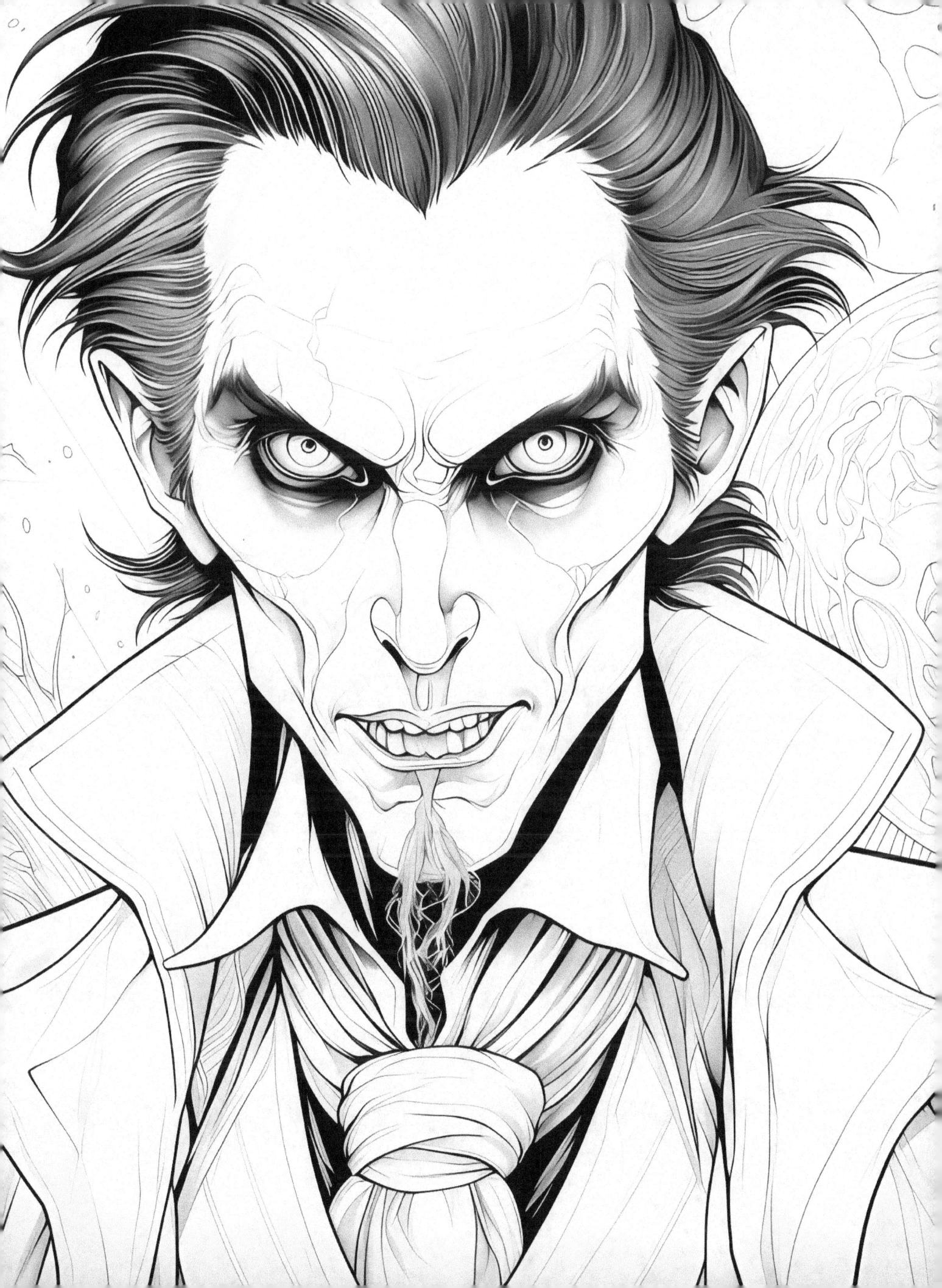

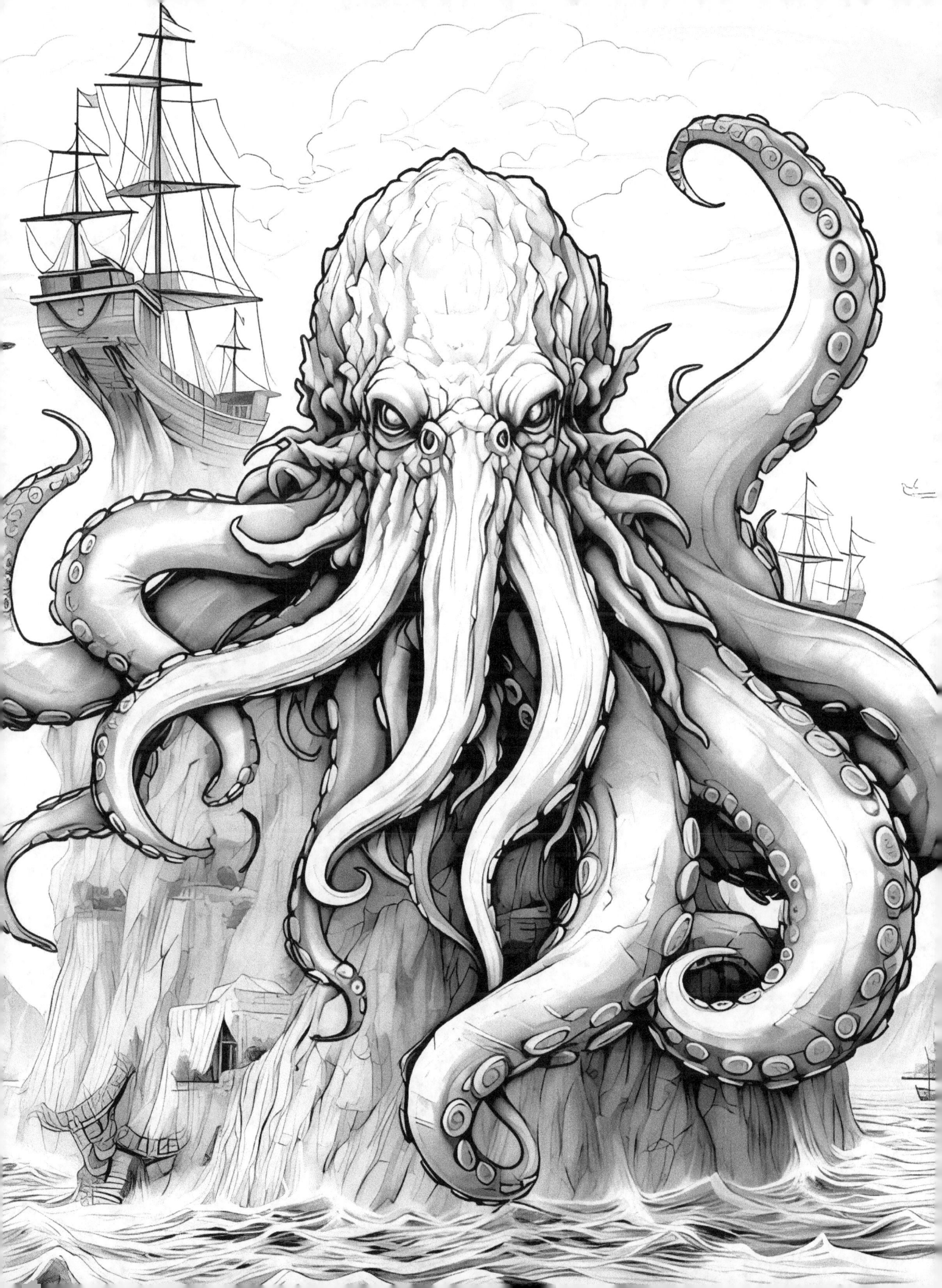

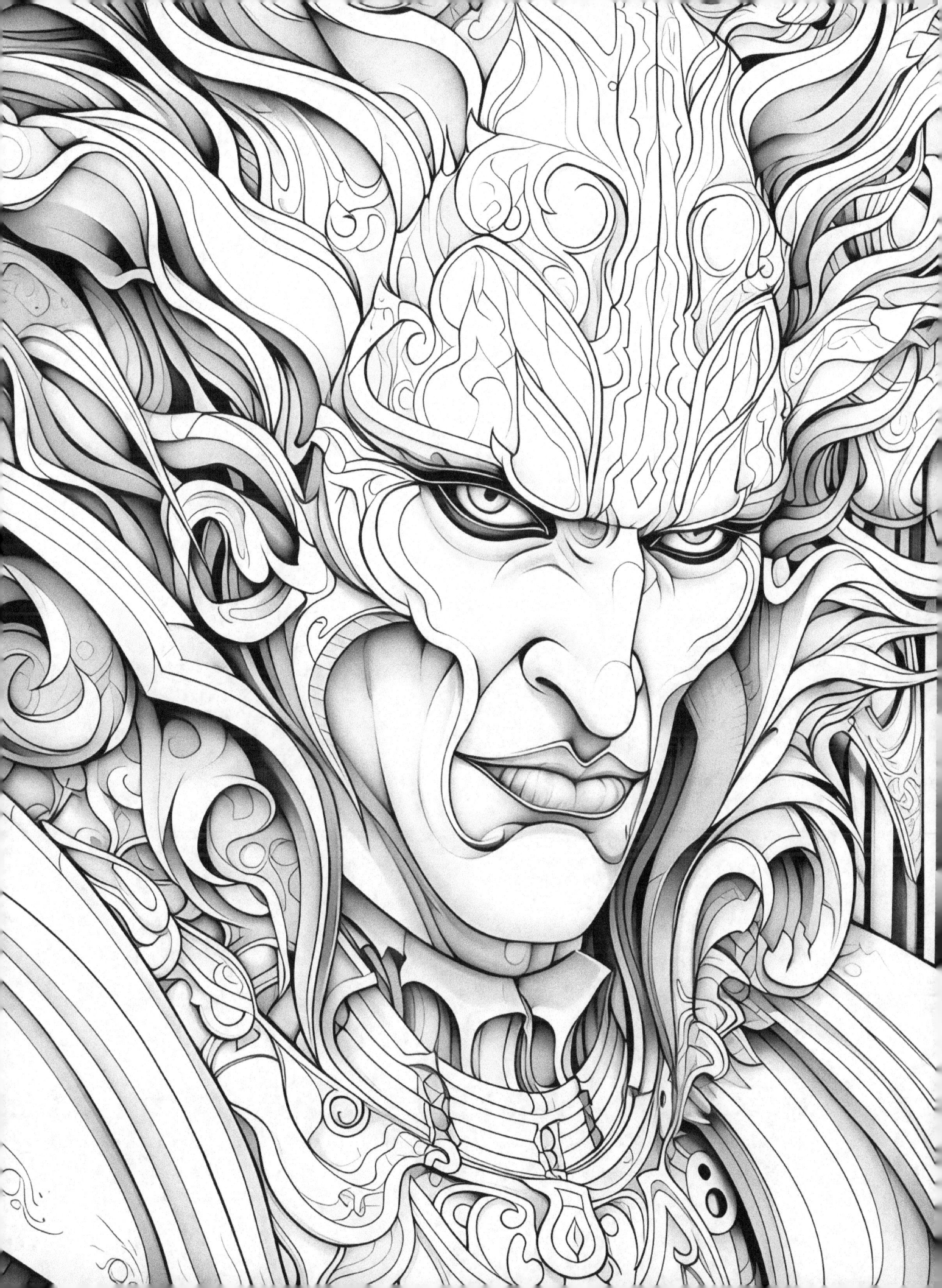

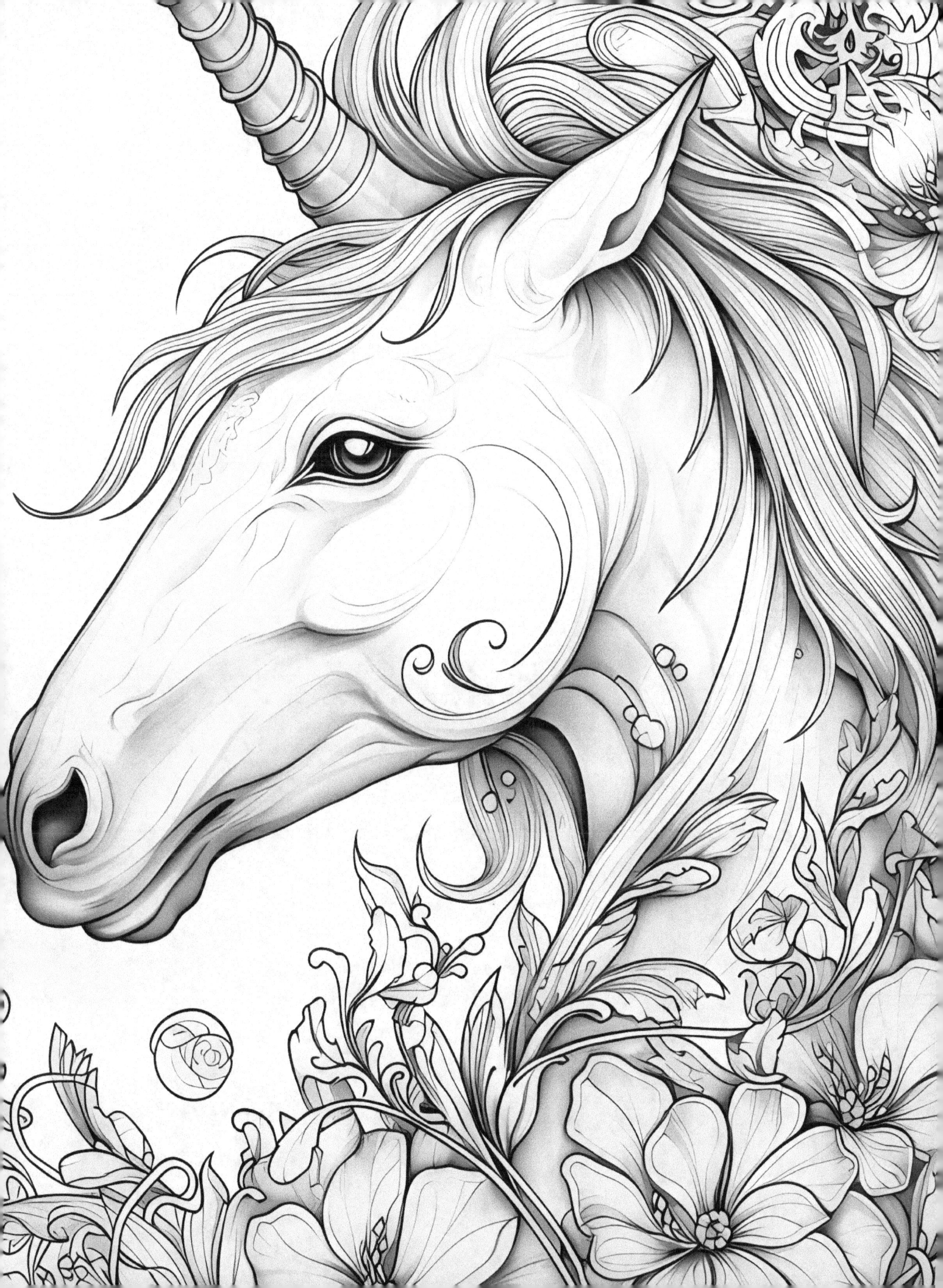

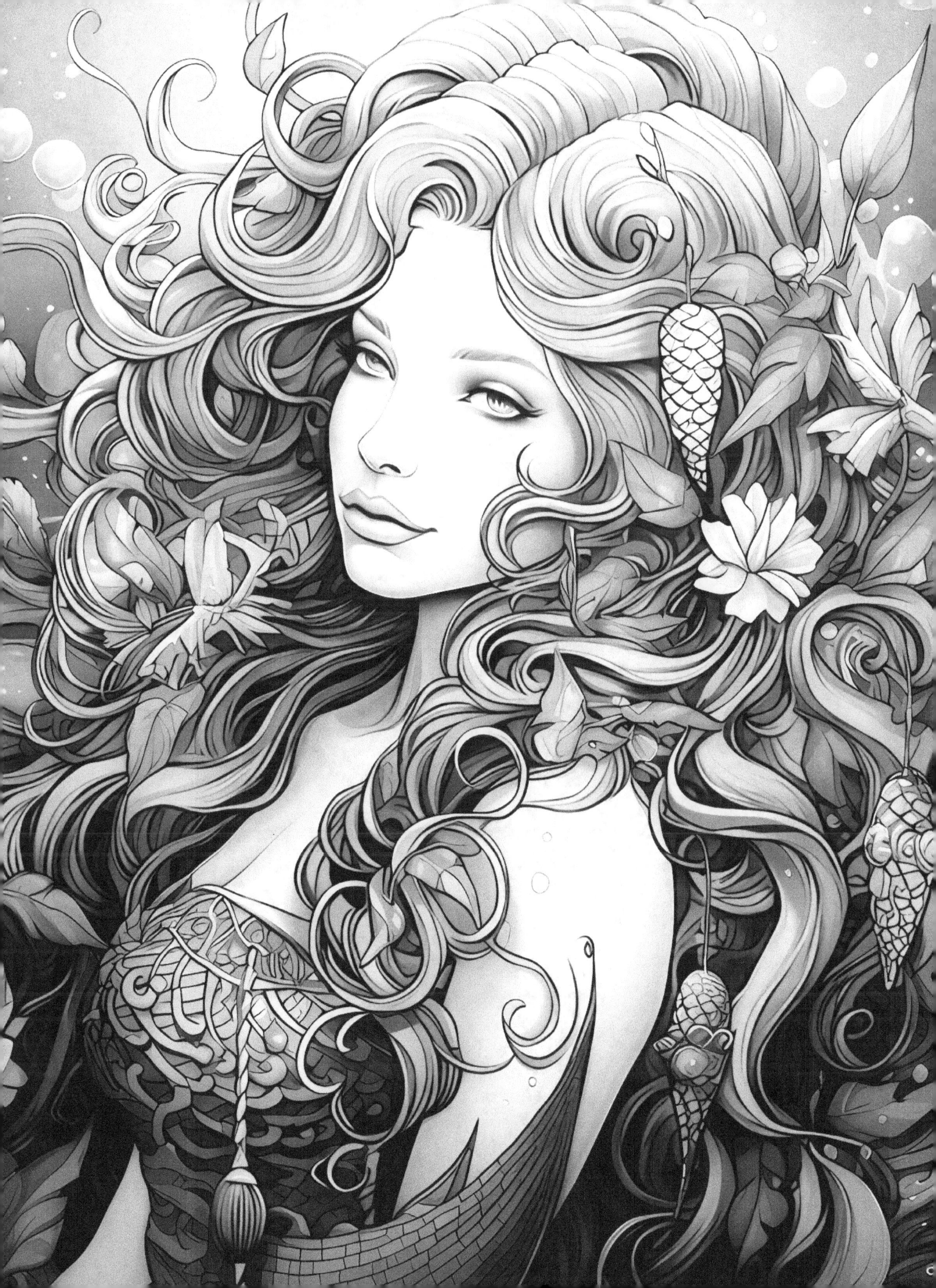

THANK YOU
FOR YOUR PURCHASE!
WE HOPE YOU ENJOY
COLORING OUR BOOK.

PLEASE LEAVE US A POSITIVE
REVIEW IF YOU ENJOYED
OUR BOOK AND POST A PICTURE
OF YOUR COLORED PAGE, OR VIDEO
WITH YOUR REVIEW.

CHECK OUT OUR OTHER
AVAILABLE BOOKS.

THANK YOU

ANGRYEYE PRESS